# BUT
## OF

STEVE WOODHALL

Published by Struik Nature
(an imprint of Random House Struik (Pty) Ltd)
Reg. No. 1966/003153/07
First Floor, Wembley Square,
Solan Road, Gardens, Cape Town, 8001
PO Box 1144, Cape Town, 8000, South Africa

Visit **www.randomstruik.co.za** and join the Struik Nature Club
for updates, news, events and special offers

First published in 2013
1 3 5 7 9 10 8 6 4 2

Copyright © in text, 2013: Steve Woodhall
Copyright © in photographs, 2013: Steve Woodhall, unless otherwise
indicated alongside photographs (see photographers' abbreviations below)
Copyright © in maps, 2013: Steve Woodhall, except where otherwise indicated
Copyright © in published edition, 2013:
Random House Struik (Pty) Ltd

Publisher: Pippa Parker
Managing editor: Helen de Villiers
Editor: Emily Bowles
Design director: Janice Evans
Design team: Tessa Fortuin, Gillian Black and Neil Bester
Proofreader: Tessa Kennedy

Reproduction by Hirt & Carter Cape (Pty) Ltd
Printed and bound by Times Offset (M) Sdn Bhd, Malaysia

All rights reserved. No part of this publication may be
reproduced, stored in a retrieval system, or transmitted,
in any form or by any means, electronic, mechanical,
photocopying, recording or otherwise without the prior
written permission of the copyright owner(s).

ISBN 978 1 92057 247 1

---

Front cover: Spotted Hairtail
Back cover, top to bottom: Aranda Copper; Brown-veined White;
Hutchinson's High-flyer; Bush Scarlet; Topaz-spotted Blue
Page 1: Broad-bordered Grass Yellow; Opposite: Autumn-leaf Vagrant

Photographers' abbreviations: AC André Coetzer; AH Alan Heath; BP Brian Plowes;
JD Jeremy Dobson; JJ John Joannou; JPB J.P. Brouard; MF Michael Field; RP Rob Paré

## ACKNOWLEDGEMENTS

This book could not have been written without the support of my wife Jayne. Thanks are due to all my friends in the Lepidopterists' Society of Africa for help, fellowship and encouragement; the photographers who loaned me images (acknowledged alongside their photographs in the book); Pippa Parker and the team at Random House Struik; Professor Les Underhill and Drs Silvia Mecenero and Colin Beale for permission to use the SABCA maps and flight period data. And last but not least the internet community at PhotoCamel for their advice on digital photography.

# CONTENTS

**Introduction** 4
What is a butterfly? 4
Butterfly anatomy 4
Butterfly early stages 5
Butterfly diversity 13
Biomes 14
Where to find butterflies 16
Recognising butterflies 18
Features of the book 18

**Species accounts** 20

**Glossary** 148

**Index to scientific names** 149

**Index to Afrikaans common names** 150

**Index to English common names** 151

# INTRODUCTION

## What is a butterfly?

Butterflies (and moths) are members of the insect order Lepidoptera. Scientists derived this name from the ancient Greek *lepidos*, meaning 'scale', and *pteron*, meaning 'wing'. The powder on the wings of these insects, seen under a microscope, is made up of tiny scales.

*Wing scales of the Red-line Sapphire, greatly magnified.*

Lepidoptera consists of 126 families grouped into 46 superfamilies. Butterflies fall within three superfamilies (two of which occur in Africa) and seven families (six in Africa). Members of the remaining families are all deemed to be moths.

Butterflies are conspicuous because they tend to be brightly coloured and diurnal. However, there are many diurnal moth species, some of which are just as spectacular as any butterfly. In fact, most people mistake them for butterflies and the distinction is largely artificial. The anatomic differences between the three butterfly superfamilies and the other 43 are the province of specialist entomologists. Popular criteria such as 'moths have feathery antennae (feelers) and butterflies clubbed', or 'moths settle with wings held flat, butterflies with wings folded' have so many exceptions as to render them meaningless. The modern answer to the question 'What's the difference between a butterfly and a moth?' is that there isn't one – they are all Lepidoptera!

This book covers 256 of South Africa's nearly 700 butterfly species, generally those that are most commonly encountered, as well as a few rarer ones.

## Butterfly anatomy

The diagrams that follow illustrate a butterfly's anatomy, wing venation and markings. The terms used in the species accounts that follow are largely straightforward, but occasionally scientific terms have been necessary to draw attention to subtle differences in colour, pattern and structure between species.

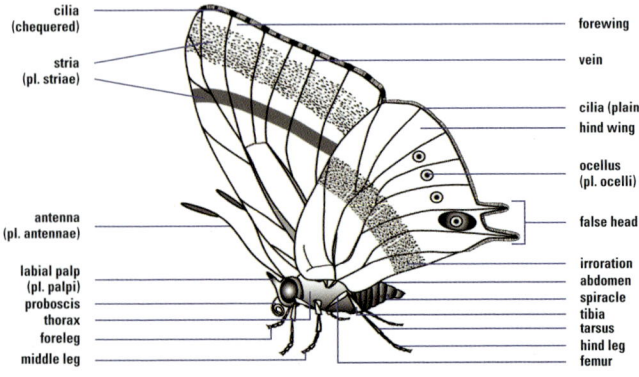

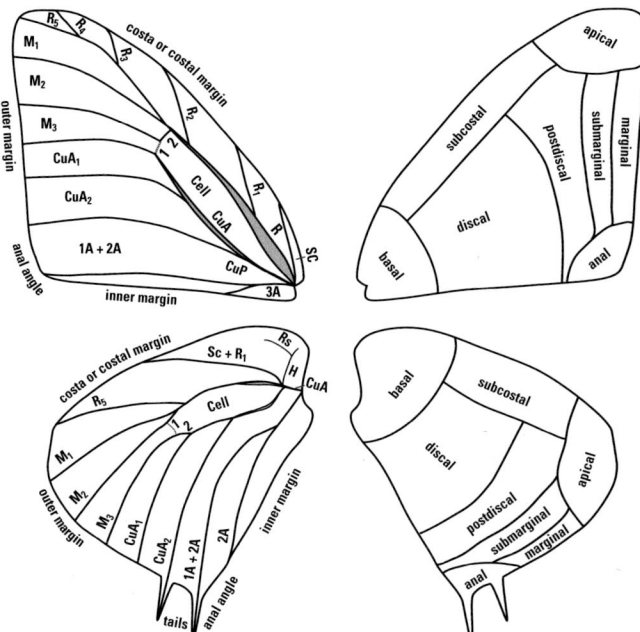

*Butterfly wing plan, indicating the veins and wing areas used to show the location of patterns and markings. Each vein names the wing area above it, as follows:* **M** = *medial vein;* **R** = *radial vein* (**Rs** = *radial sector vein);* **CuA** = *anterior cubital veins;* **CuP** = *posterior cubital vein;* **A** = *anal veins;* **H** = *humeral vein;* **Sc** = *subcostal vein;* (**1A+2A**) *and (***Sc+R$_1$***) = composite veins.* **(Many of these terms don't appear in the accounts, but the detailed sketch is provided for interested readers.)**

Like all insects, butterflies have six legs and four wings. Their wings comprise thin skins held taut by the veins. Body fluids travel along these veins, helping to keep the insect warm. Unlike vertebrates, insects do not have blood. Rather, their internal parts are bathed in a liquid known as *haemolymph*, which carries nutrients (but not oxygen) to the organs. A butterfly respires via *spiracles* on the sides of its body that allow oxygen to diffuse directly into the tissues.

The body consists of the head, thorax and abdomen. All the limbs are attached to the abdomen. The head bears the eyes, antennae, scent-detecting organs (the labial palpi) and feeding tube (proboscis). With the exception of a few primitive moths, Lepidoptera lack biting mouthparts.

## Butterfly early stages

Like wasps, flies and beetles, among others, a Lepidopteran's life cycle comprises four distinct stages: egg (*ovum*, plural *ova*), caterpillar (*larva*, plural *larvae*), chrysalis (*pupa*, plural *pupae*) and adult (*imago*, plural *imagines*). Each stage is quite distinct from the others, offering little indication as to how the individual may look in the next stage. Other insects like grasshoppers, bugs and dragonflies hatch into tiny nymphs closely resembling the adults, and then go through successive moults as they grow to full size.

The following examples of eggs, larvae and pupae typify the main butterfly subfamilies, showing the extent to which early life stages vary between species.

## Eggs

Butterfly eggs vary as much in size and form as do the adults. Different species within a family or subfamily tend to have similar eggs. The eggs shown in the photographs below are of a species whose eggs are typical for its family or subfamily.

African Monarch

### Nymphalidae – Danainae
Danaine eggs are oval and pointed with slender vertical ribs and cross-ribbing. They are usually laid singly (one at a time, alone) but some species lay small batches of 3–6 eggs, each about 1.5 mm high.

Common Bush Brown

### Nymphalidae – Satyrinae
Among certain Satyrine species, the females simply scatter their eggs into the grass as they fly. These eggs tend to be rounded and featureless, like the one shown here. In other species, females cement their eggs to a grass stem. In such cases the eggs are generally more elongated with fine longitudinal ribbing.

Dusky-veined Acraea

### Nymphalidae – Heliconiinae
Heliconiinae of the genera *Acraea* and *Telchinia* tend to lay their eggs in batches. Each batch may number hundreds of eggs, laid in double and even triple layers, like the batch shown here. Other Heliconiinae such as butterflies in the genus *Phalanta* lay their eggs singly.

Pearl Charaxes

### Nymphalidae – Charaxinae
*Charaxes* are large butterflies, and their eggs reflect this – some are more than 2 mm across. The eggs are always rounded with a more or less flat crown, sometimes with radiating flutes. A fertile egg develops a dark circlet, as is evident on the egg shown here.

Gold-banded Forester

### Nymphalidae – Limenitinae
Limenitine species lay their eggs singly. These eggs often have a honeycombed appearance with many tiny bristles arising from the edges of each facet. Initially green, the egg develops red rings if fertile and then turns black as the larva forms inside.

Common Mother-of-Pearl

### Nymphalidae – Nymphalinae
Nymphalinae eggs are remarkably similar in shape and design. Although the adult butterflies in this subfamily are very different in shape, their eggs can scarcely be told apart. They are typically domed with prominent vertical ribbing.

Amakosa Rocksitter

### Lycaenidae – Poritiinae
Lycaenid eggs are less diverse in shape than those of the Nymphalids. Most are tiny pill- or pastille-shaped domes with facets or finely chiselled cross-ribbing. This egg has been laid on a rock close to the lichen that the larva will feed on.

INTRODUCTION

### Lycaenidae – Miletinae
The pill-shaped eggs of Miletinae are typical of the family Lycaenidae. Eggs of the genus *Thestor* (the skollies) are instantly recognisable by the tiny bulge on one side, clearly visible on the egg shown here. The female lays her eggs singly or in small batches, close to their prey, or even in bare earth near the pathways of their host ant species. It is not certain whether the ants carry the eggs into their nests.

Basuto Skolly

### Lycaenidae – Theclinae
Thecline eggs have quite variable surface patterns. The eggs of the Common Fig-tree Blue shown here have deep facets and a pronounced sponge-like appearance. Other species in the subfamily have facets that are far smaller, or that are shallow, something like the surface of a golf ball.

Common Fig-tree Blue

### Lycaenidae – Polyommatinae
This is a good example of a Polyommatine egg. Tiny (less than 0.5 mm across) and pill-shaped, it has an intricate tracery of cross-ribbing. Tiny knobs mark the points where the cross-ribs meet.

Pea Blue

### Pieridae – Pierinae
Pierid eggs are usually bottle- or skittle-shaped and may be laid singly or, like the ones shown here, in groups. In those species that lay batches, the larvae tend to be gregarious and remain together until pupation.

African Common White

### Papilionidae
Swallowtail and swordtail eggs, like that of the Citrus Swallowtail shown here, are large, spherical and featureless and are usually yellow to pale green. The female cements her eggs to a plant with a sticky secretion. Like some Nymphalid eggs, swallowtail eggs develop dark marks if they are fertile.

Citrus Swallowtail

### Hesperiidae – Coeliadinae
Most skipper eggs are domed with vertical ribs, like those seen on this Red-tab Policeman's egg. They are laid singly or in pairs, and darken if fertile, usually just before the young larva hatches out.

Red-tab Policeman

### Hesperiidae – Pyrginae
Pyrgine eggs are also domed and ribbed, but in many species this is seldom seen, because the female covers the eggs with hairs transferred from the tip of her abdomen. The hairs probably serve as a protective barrier against small parasitic wasps that may lay their own eggs inside the butterfly's egg, killing the larva.

Clouded Flat

## Larvae

The time taken for larvae to reach full size varies greatly. Some go from egg to adult in just weeks. Others take almost a year. The time can vary according to the species, or depending on rainfall. Full-grown butterfly caterpillars are amazingly diverse. Some look nothing like their earlier phases (instars), but larvae within each family will share certain common features. The following are just a few examples to illustrate the range.

African Monarch

**Nymphalidae – Danainae**
Danaine larvae feed on poisonous plants and have conspicuous aposematic (warning) colours. Other members of the subfamily have larvae that are shiny and black with bright spots and stripes.

Common Bush Brown

**Nymphalidae – Satyrinae**
The larvae of browns and ringlets feed almost exclusively on grasses and sedges. Brown or green in colour, these larvae usually hide by day at the base of a clump of grass, emerging at night to feed. Some montane species, like widows, take an entire year to attain their adult size.

Dusky-veined Acraea

**Nymphalidae – Heliconiinae**
Many Heliconiine larvae are gregarious. They feed on poisonous plants and are harmful to most birds, so it may be that their spines and gregarious behaviour serve as a warning. Non-toxic Biblidine larvae are very similar, as are some Nymphalines, possibly both cases of defensive mimicry.

Forest Queen

**Nymphalidae – Charaxinae**
The larva shown here is an extreme example of a Charaxine caterpillar – it resembles a nibbled leaf with withered white edges. All Charaxine larvae have extensive head horns and some ornamentation on the back. The tail is usually bifid (divided in two). Seemingly conspicuous, they are in fact well camouflaged.

False Wanderer

**Nymphalidae – Limenitinae**
Caterpillars of this subfamily are variable. Sailers and false acraeas are fantastically shaped and carry horns; foresters and guinea-fowl have long feathery spines on their sides, while glider larvae are spiny and resemble Heliconiines.

## Nymphalidae – Nymphalinae

Nymphaline larvae typically have long branched spines and, in many species, also carry a pair of spines on the head, as does the larva shown here. Heliconiine and Biblidine larvae also have branched spines. The spines make Nymphaline larvae look rather like poisonous Heliconiine larvae, so perhaps they help to trick birds into leaving these caterpillars alone.

**Variable Diadem**

## Lycaenidae – Poritiinae

All Poritiine larvae feed on lichen. Rocksitters and Zulus favour rock lichen, and so their larvae are moderately hairy and well camouflaged against the rocks on which they find their food. Buffs' larvae feed on tree lichen, have extremely long hairs and are even more difficult to find.

**Amakosa Rocksitter**

## Lycaenidae – Miletinae

Miletine larvae are non-herbivorous. The life cycle of the skollies is poorly documented. In some skolly species, the young larvae feed on scale insects, while the older larvae are found in the nests of pugnacious (*Anaplolepis*) ants. In other species, including the Peninsula Skolly shown here, ants have been observed feeding the larva, rather as a host bird can be tricked into feeding a cuckoo chick. Woolly Legs (also Miletinae) larvae feed on aphids and scale insects, but do not enter ant nests.

**Peninsula Skolly**

## Lycaenidae – Theclinae

Thecline larvae are typically slug-shaped, like the Natal Opal caterpillar shown here being attended to by cocktail (*Crematogaster*) ants. The ants are attracted to the larva because it exudes chemicals that mimic ant pheromones. These fool them into treating the larva as one of their own brood. Butterflies in this subfamily are diverse in appearance, but their larvae tend to look very much alike.

**Natal Opal**

## Lycaenidae – Polyommatinae

Polyommatinae, known as blues, have slug-like caterpillars that often feed on plant seeds and young growth shoots – protein-rich food that facilitates the rapid larval growth typical in this family. Lycaeninae larvae are very similar, but feed mainly on leaves.

**Common Zebra Blue**

**Veined Tip**

### Pieridae – Pierinae
Pierid larvae, with their extraordinary countershading, are beautifully camouflaged and may be solitary or gregarious. Although they hide very effectively, evidence suggests they have additional defences. For example, it seems that some sequester foul-smelling mustard oils from their food plants, and use them to deter predators.

**Emperor Swallowtail**

### Papilionidae
In both swallowtails and swordtails the larva is cylindrical and hairless. The part corresponding to the adult's thorax, the prothorax, is thickened. This often carries small eyespots. When alarmed, the larva puffs itself up, squirms from side to side and extrudes a forked organ (visible here) called an *osmaterium*, which emits an offensive scent and makes the larva resemble a small snake.

**Red-tab Policeman**

### Hesperiidae – Coeliadinae
All Hesperiid (skipper) larvae hide inside shelters made from leaves stitched together. Policemen are noted for their brightly coloured, hoop-striped larvae, which superficially resemble monarch larvae, possibly for protection.

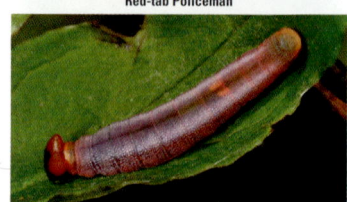
**Clouded Flat**

### Hesperiidae – Pyrginae
Most skipper larvae are brown to green, but some are red or purple, like the Clouded Flat larva shown here. Note the 'neck' just behind the head, a characteristic feature of all skipper larvae.

## Pupae

Butterfly pupae (or chrysalides) are also variable. When the caterpillar is fully grown, it senses the need to form a pupa (to *pupate*), seeks out a suitable spot and begins its preparations. Some form inside a shelter; some, like this Blue Pansy, pupate hanging by the tail from a silken pad; still others spin a silk girdle around themselves and pupate horizontally. After a few days the final moult reveals the new pupa.

The images that follow show a representative selection of butterfly pupae.

*This Blue Pansy larva is in the early stages of pupation.*

INTRODUCTION

**Nymphalidae – Danainae**
This Chief pupa well illustrates the mirror-like sheen seen on many Danaine pupae. The pupae of African Monarchs, the most common Danainae, lack this sheen. They are plain white, green or blue. Reflective markings probably provide camouflage. Although it looks garish in this photograph, in the wild the pupa takes on the colours of its surroundings and vanishes into the background.

Chief

**Nymphalidae – Satyrinae**
Like all Nymphalids, Satyrines pupate head-down. The tail tip is covered in tiny hooks, which entangle with a silk pad spun on the substrate by the larva, rather like Velcro. Bush brown pupae are highly variable and range in colour from yellow to green to chocolate brown.

Common Bush Brown

**Nymphalidae – Heliconiinae**
Like the Common Leopard pupa shown here, many Heliconiine pupae have fantastic spines, excrescences and metallic marks. The pupae seem gaudy, but are almost impossible to spot among the leaves of their food plants. Bitter Acraea pupae often form in the open, as their aposematic colours protect them from predators.

Common Leopard

**Nymphalidae – Charaxinae**
Emperor pupae are generally similar to one another. Their resemblance to curled-up leaves provides them with protection. Many, like the Silver-barred Charaxes pupa shown here, are plain green, but some have pale markings and lines that help to break up their outline, making them even more difficult to spot.

Silver-barred Charaxes

**Nymphalidae – Limenitinae**
Like their larvae, Limenitine pupae are extremely variable. Many, like the Blonde Glider pupa in this photograph, have sharply creased ridges on their backs. False acraea pupae resemble the long, thin, immature leaves of their food plants, while foresters and sailers have spectacular metallic spots that provide camouflage.

Blonde Glider

**Nymphalidae – Nymphalinae**
The shape of the pupae shown here is typical for Nymphalines. This is the character by which they are best identified, since the pupae vary in size and in the extent to which their protuberances are embellished with spines and metallic spots. This variation is seen even within a species. For example, the Soldier Pansy pupae featured here came from the eggs of a single female.

Soldier Pansy

Yellow Zulu

**Lycaenidae – Poritiinae**
Like the larvae, Poritiine pupae are hairy and rounded. They are usually concealed under rocks or tree bark and, like most Lycaenids, are attached by the tail and a silk midriff girdle.

Southern Pied Woolly Legs

**Lycaenidae – Miletinae**
This is a rare photograph of a *Lachnocnema* pupa. The larvae prey on aphids and plant lice, and are very well hidden. The pupa forms some distance from the aphid colony, presumably to protect it from the ants attending the aphids.

Saffron Sapphire

**Lycaenidae – Theclinae**
Unlike many Theclinae, sapphire pupae are not formed in an ants' nest. Instead, they usually form on the bark of a tree near to a food plant, as was the case with this Saffron Sapphire pupa. Pupae in this group are usually attached by a silk tail pad with no girdle. *Iolaus* pupae are noted for their camouflage, but can be found by spraying the bark with chilled water, which (for reasons not fully understood) causes them to tap the bark, giving themselves away.

Black-striped Hairtail

**Lycaenidae – Polyommatinae**
Hairtails feed out in the open on young foliage, relying on their protective markings to hide them from the predator's gaze. This Black-striped Hairtail pupa has diagonal stripes that line up with the leaflets of the *Acacia* that it eats, thus breaking up its outline.

Broad-bordered Grass Yellow

**Pieridae – Coeliadinae**
Pierids, like Papilionids and most Lycaenids, attach their pupae via a silk tail pad and a thoracic girdle. Most Coeliadines pupae are slender, like this Broad-bordered Grass Yellow. Grass yellows pupate low down on the stems of their food plants, among dense vegetation, and are very hard to find unless bred from an egg, like the one featured here.

Buquet's Vagrant

**Pieridae – Pierinae**
Pierine pupae, like the Buquet's Vagrant pupa shown here, often have expanded, pronounced wing cases. The pupa closely resembles the leaf of a food plant, which renders it almost invisible even when out in the open. In arid conditions the pupae are usually buff-coloured, which blends in well with dry vegetation.

**Papilionidae**
Swallowtail and swordtail pupae are distinguished from Pierids by their (generally) larger size and their squared-off or bifid, rather than pointed, heads. Their colour is variable and seems to depend on the colour of the surrounding foliage.

**Green-banded Swallowtail**

**Hesperiidae – Coeliadinae**
Policeman pupae form inside the leaf shelters constructed by the larvae. Like those of many skippers, these pupae are covered in a whitish powder, the function of which is unknown. Policemen do not spin a cocoon, although they do spin a silk girdle like those spun by swallowtails and Pierids.

**Striped Policeman**

**Hesperiidae – Hesperiinae**
Nightfighters are as close to moths as butterflies get. Like other skippers, these larvae live inside shelters made from leaves stitched together, and they spin cocoons inside which to pupate, which conflicts with the conventional wisdom that only moths spin cocoons. Here a cocoon has been broken open, revealing the pupa inside.

**Palm-tree Nightfighter**

## Butterfly diversity

South Africa is home to more than 670 butterfly species – a substantial number for a country that lies largely outside of the tropics. In recent years, many birders have taken to 'ticking' butterflies too. The hobby is particularly rewarding given the wide range of species found here, which vary enormously both in size (from the tiniest blues and coppers to the biggest swallowtails and emperors) and in colour (from dull brown to flashy spectacular metallic tones). Many species are endemic to South Africa, being found nowhere else in the world. An experienced birder is generally able to distinguish between even the most nondescript 'little brown jobs', if only by a single feature, but watching butterflies provides a further challenge, since many species are so similar that they are only reliably distinguished with a microscope.

The recent South African Butterfly Conservation Assessment (SABCA) was a four-year project aimed at determining the distribution and conservation status of all southern African butterfly species. A collaboration between the South African National Biodiversity Institute, the Animal Demography Unit of the University of Cape Town, the Lepidopterists' Society of Africa and various citizen science projects, this was the first scientific assessment of all the region's butterflies geographically and over time.

**Polka Dot**

The data gathered was used to produce maps showing both the distribution of each butterfly and the statistical likelihood of its being found in a particular place. The maps and flight period bars given in this pocket guide draw on this data, representing a very accurate digest of sightings per month over many years.

## Biomes

The term *biome* is used to describe the type of climate and dominant plants and animals that occur in a particular area.

Note that patches of vegetation typical of one biome frequently occur inside another biome. Here we describe the main biomes in the region, highlighting the butterflies most closely associated with each.

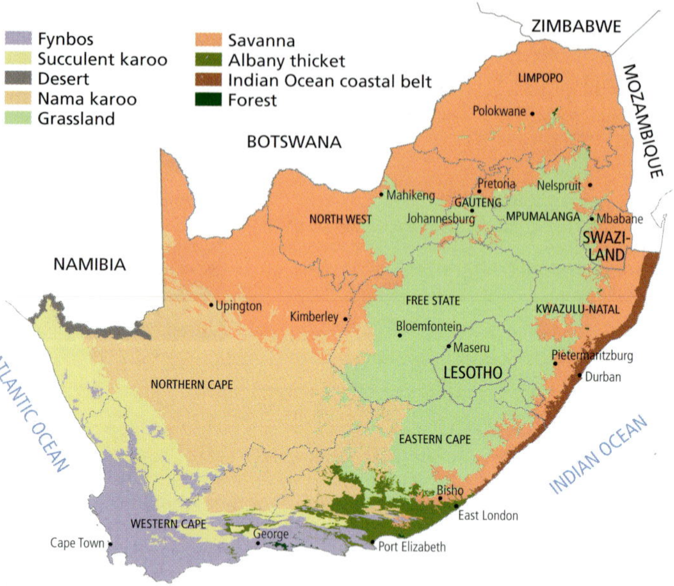

- Fynbos
- Succulent karoo
- Desert
- Nama karoo
- Grassland
- Savanna
- Albany thicket
- Indian Ocean coastal belt
- Forest

*South Africa's biomes (from* The Vegetation of South Africa, Lesotho and Swaziland *(2006), by kind permission of the South African National Biodiversity Institute and L. Mucina & M.C. Rutherford (eds.).)*

### Fynbos

South Africa's most celebrated biome, fynbos is remarkable for its floristic diversity. It comprises two main vegetation types – true fynbos, found on hills, valleys and mountains, and the endangered renosterveld, which grows along the coast. Many endemic butterflies occur here, mostly blues, coppers and browns. Species are often confined to small areas and are difficult, but very rewarding, to find. Many of the region's most endangered butterflies occur in the fynbos biome.

### Succulent karoo

Found along the Atlantic coast and its inland mountain ranges, this biome includes pockets of fynbos. Succulent dwarf shrubs are typical and grasses are rare. Many people visit Namaqualand in spring to see the flowers, and this is also the season to look for some very special butterflies, including many endemics. Namaqualand's butterflies have much in common with fynbos and Nama karoo species. Finding mountain-dwelling species generally requires some strenuous climbing.

## Desert

In South Africa true desert occurs only in the extreme northwest, along the Orange River valley. The sparse vegetation here is adapted for very arid conditions. The few butterflies are mainly those typical of savanna and Nama karoo, and occur along river courses. A few desert specialists occur in Namibia, of which one or two also occur in South Africa.

## Nama karoo

Dwarf shrubs and sparse hard grasses characterise the western central plateau of South Africa. The butterflies here are similar to those found in fynbos. They include many endemics, but are hard to find as they tend to live in small pockets with special microclimates. Search in dense vegetation along river courses, or along mountain ridges.

## Grassland

Grassland typifies the eastern central plateau of South Africa. This habitat has largely been transformed by maize farming, but some true grassland areas still survive along the hills south of Johannesburg. The best places to search for grassland butterflies are on the eastern Drakensberg and Wolkberg escarpments and on the Lesotho plateau. These areas are home to several rare and specialised species.

## Savanna

Savanna is our largest biome. It is moist in the north and east of South Africa, but arid in the west, where it blends with Nama karoo and desert. Typically it consists of a grassy lower layer with stands of dense or scattered trees and shrubs. The butterflies here are mainly widespread species or species closely related to those occurring to the north, but there are also small populations of specialist endemics.

## Albany thicket

This short, dense, woodland vegetation is better adapted to arid conditions than true forest. It includes fewer grasses than savanna, but is less arid than Nama karoo. Butterflies here are also typically found in the Nama karoo to the south and west, although forest and savanna species penetrate Albany thicket in the north. Few endemics occur here. This harsh, spiny, often impenetrable vegetation makes for interesting butterflying.

## Indian Ocean coastal belt

A narrow belt of coastal vegetation that also penetrates inland along deep valleys. It is characterised by thick bush. In the south and central areas, this biome is under threat from mining and farming. Some areas are well preserved, for example at Kosi Bay, but the Zululand flats are threatened by subsistence agriculture and human settlement. The butterflies here are similar to those found along the littoral as far as Kenya, with just a few special endemics.

## Forest

Forest is our smallest biome. The scattered patches of indigenous forest that remain are threatened by water starvation resulting from extensive exotic plantations. Forests may be Afrotemperate, lowland or riverine. The Afrotemperate type is home to many endemics, while lowland and riverine forests often harbour species also found in tropical Africa. The forests of northeastern Limpopo are richer in butterfly species than any other forested area in our region.

# Where to find butterflies

Some butterflies occur across several, or all, biomes. Others, the fascinating specialists, are found in one biome only, and often just within a tiny area of that biome.

While butterflying is a great way to get you out into South Africa's wild and beautiful places, you don't have to go too far afield to get started.

## Gardens

Increasingly, gardeners are planting the indigenous species that attract butterflies. A large well-established garden with trees, shrubs and locally indigenous flowers is a great place to find butterflies. Although wild females must lay their eggs on their natural food plants, the nectar that adults feed on need not be indigenous. Even an exotic alien like Cherry Pie *Lantana camara* can be an excellent source of nectar.

*This established indigenous garden in KwaZulu-Natal was planted specifically to attract butterflies.*

## Roadsides

Because they tend not to be cultivated, and thus inadvertently preserve the last remnants of wild habitat, road verges are often surprisingly rich in butterflies. In addition, authorities may cut back roadside bush or scrub to improve visibility, allowing flowering plants to thrive. In the savanna areas north of the Soutpansberg, good autumn rains herald great butterflying, as run-off from the road results in luxuriant plant growth. Flowers like *Vernonia centauroides* attract thousands of butterflies, usually Pieridae (which includes the whites, tips and yellows), as well as a sprinkling of butterflies from other families. Days may be spent here with a fresh surprise awaiting you on each clump of flowers.

## Hilltops

For those with the energy to climb, or who can find a mountain with a handy road to its summit, the peaks of koppies, ridges and crags are great places to see butterflies. This is because, among many butterfly species that occur at low density, the males have evolved to congregate at prominent points, such as tall trees, rocks and hilltops. Here they vie for the best vantage points from which to pursue females that come up the hill later in the day in search of mates. This gathering of competing males in a 'lek' territory – a kind of real life king-of-the-castle game – will be familiar to many birders.

Some species rise to the summits as early as 08h00; others wait longer, sometimes delaying until the late afternoon. A day out on a hilltop can therefore be a rewarding experience with different butterflies coming up every hour.

*Thousands of Brown-veined Whites occur on* Vernonia *flowers north of the Soutpansberg.*

*This Giant Charaxes was found on a high hilltop early one morning in Hluhluwe-iMfolozi Park, KwaZulu-Natal.*

## Forests

The image of a butterfly-filled tropical rainforest is rightly something of a cliché, only reinforced by butterfly flight houses with their lush vegetation, steamy conditions and myriad butterflies. These exhibits are a wonderful experience, especially for those who aren't lucky enough to live close to a real tropical forest. South Africa does have tropical forests – fewer and less extensive than those in Central and West Africa – but enough to give you the real experience.

Butterflies are highly seasonal. No matter where you are in the world, the best time to visit a tropical forest is just after the rains. Even in the Amazon you'll see hardly any butterflies if you visit at the wrong time of the year. The same is true of forests in South Africa. At the height of summer they can be almost butterfly-free. But in late summer, autumn and even winter forests may be teeming with butterflies.

In our region, the best forests in which to view butterflies are the lowland forests in the north and east and along the east coast. Further south, the diversity of species and number of butterflies declines, and the same is true of increasing altitude. Although there are some beautiful high-altitude forests in South Africa, none is as rich in butterfly species as the lowland forests of Zululand and northeastern Limpopo.

*Butterflying in high-altitude Afrotemperate forest at Qhudeni, KwaZulu-Natal; this is one of the best places to see our largest butterfly, the Emperor Swallowtail.*

## Wetlands

Mossy bogs, riversides and vleis are often better places to find butterflies than the surrounding grassland or savanna habitat. This is because wetlands frequently host a greater variety of flowering plants, herbs and grasses that are suitable food plants for butterfly larvae.

Many interesting butterflies are specialised for life in wetland habitats, especially wetlands at high altitude in grassland patches. Here, the surrounding vegetation may show little plant and butterfly diversity, but the marsh will reward a patient observer. Wellington boots or waders may be necessary.

*This high-altitude marshy stream is home to specialist butterflies like the Marsh Mountain Blue.*

## Mud puddles

Most butterflies are herbivores. The larvae eat plants and the adults drink nectar, a diet that lacks salts and minerals and therefore needs augmentation, just like the diet of an antelope, for example. A water-hole is the perfect place to do this and, consequently, an excellent spot to view butterflies. Not only do the insects swarm here to drink in hot weather, but they also come to absorb salts and minerals at the places where animals have urinated on the mud. Even human urine is a powerful lure, a trick that butterfly collectors have long employed. Other good sources of salts include animal and bird droppings and weathered bones.

*A Veined Swordtail and a Green-banded Swallowtail on a puddle of urine-soaked mud.*

## Recognising butterflies

This pocket-sized book is designed to help you identify common butterflies in the field. The more difficult groups are not covered comprehensively, but you should be able to narrow down the subfamily to which a given butterfly belongs so that you can later refer to a fuller reference to establish the species.

It may be helpful to page through the book at your leisure, familiarising yourself with the various types of butterfly. When in the field, use the book along with this six-point identification checklist to help you identify a specimen:

- How big is it (in relation to those butterflies you already know)?
- What shape are its wings and what is its resting posture?
- What is its overall colour?
- What kind of markings does it have?
- How is it behaving? What is its 'jizz'?
- Finally, have you checked the distribution map to see if the species you think you're looking at does in fact occur in the area?

*Female Eyed Pansy drinking nectar. Her wings-open position is typical for a pansy butterfly.*

## Features of the book

1. **MAP** A guide to the entire likely range of the species, based on the latest South African Butterfly Conservation Assessment data (see p. 13).
2. **GROUP NAME** The common, family and subfamily names for the group.
3. **SPECIES NAME** English and Afrikaans common names and latest scientific name of each species. Common names vary regionally and change over time. The only name guaranteed to be unique to each species or subspecies is the scientific name, as controlled by the International Convention on Zoological Nomenclature. Scientific names can change only when a paper is published in a peer-reviewed journal. There are no such rules controlling common names. Those given here agree with the names used in the Animal Demography Unit's Virtual Museum, and differ slightly from previous books written by this author.
4. **PHOTOGRAPHS** The upper- and undersides, as well as male and female upper sides in the case of sexually dimorphic species. For butterflies with more than one subspecies, the image shows the nominate, unless otherwise indicated. If the sexes are similar, only one sex may be shown. Many butterflies are polymorphic, meaning there are several different colour or pattern forms. Those that have official names are indicated, but not all wet and dry season forms have such names. Space constraints preclude showing all forms of butterflies that are highly polymorphic.
5. **SIZE RANGE** An average range for both sexes, measured from wingtip to wingtip across the thorax.
6. **DESCRIPTION** Habits, habitat, what is known of the species' early stages, typical variation, similar species and abundance. All species are assumed to be of Least Concern on the red data list, unless otherwise stated.
7. **CALENDAR BAR** Likelihood of encountering butterfly, as a percentage of annual records ☐ = 0–2% of annual records ☐ = 3–14% of annual records ☐ = 15–39% of annual records ☐ = peak emergence >40%.

## African Monarch
Melkboskoenlapper
*Danaus chrysippus orientis*  50–75 mm

**HABITS** Flies slowly, settling often for nectar. Males may swarm on injured or wilted plants that exude alkaloids. **HABITAT** Found in most habitats, but favours open country. **EARLY STAGES** *Egg* oval and faintly ribbed. Cream-white. Laid singly on a shoot of the food plant *Gomphorcarpus fruticosus* or any of the Apocynaceae. *Larva* up to 50 mm. Cylindrical. Conspicuous. White with black and yellow hoops and long, flexible black filament. *Pupa* up to 20 mm. Cream to pale green. Hangs head-down from a leaf or stem. **VARIATION** Sexes similar, but ♂ lacks large black spot in CuA2 of hind wing. **SIMILAR SPECIES** Several mimics including ♀ Common Diadem (p. 62) and ♀ Mocker Swallowtail form *trophonius* (p. 127). **STATUS** Common and widespread.

J F M A M J J A S O N D

## Friar
Monnik
*Amauris niavius dominicanus*  75–82 mm

**HABITS** Slow, high, sailing flight. Settles often, but easily disturbed. Fond of flowers. Males may swarm on injured or wilted plants that exude alkaloids. **HABITAT** Lowland and riverine forest and surrounding disturbed areas. **EARLY STAGES** Not recorded, but likely to resemble those of Novice (p. 21). Larva known to feed on *Cynanchum* and *Tylophora* lianas (Apocynaceae). **VARIATION** Sexes similar, but ♂ has grey sex mark at anal angle of hind wing. **SIMILAR SPECIES** Several mimics including ♀ Forest Queen (p. 54), ♀ Mocker Swallowtail form *trophonius* (p. 127) and Variable Diadem form *wahlbergi* (p. 62). **STATUS** Locally common.

J F M A M J J A S O N D

## Novice
**Outannie**
*Amauris ochlea ochlea*        **55–65 mm**

**HABITS** Slow sailing flight. Settles often, but wary. Fond of flowers. Males may swarm on wilted plants that exude alkaloids. **HABITAT** Forest, coastal woodlands and surrounding disturbed areas. **EARLY STAGES** *Egg* upright, pointed, faintly ribbed. Cream-white. Laid singly under a leaf of *Cynanchum*, *Tylophora* or another of the forest Apocynaceae. *Larva* up to 40 mm. Shape and filaments similar to those of an African Monarch larva. Jet black with white spots. *Pupa* up to 20 m. Buff with golden mirror-like panels. Hangs head-down from a leaf. **VARIATION** Sexes similar, but ♂ has grey sex brand at anal angle of hind wing. **SIMILAR SPECIES** Main mimic is Deceptive Diadem (KZN to E. Cape coast). **STATUS** Locally common.

J F M A M J J A S O N D

---

## Layman
**Ouheks**
*Amauris albimaculata albimaculata*      **50–68 mm**

**HABITS** Slow, lazy, usually high flight. Descends to feed on flowers. Males may swarm on damaged or wilted plants to imbibe alkaloids. **HABITAT** Forest. **EARLY STAGES** *Egg* a ribbed oval. Cream-white. Laid in clusters of 3–40, under the leaf of a food plant like *Cynanchum*, *Tylophora* or another of the forest Apocynaceae. *Larva* up to 36 mm. Shape and filaments similar to those of an African Monarch larva. Grey-black with rows of yellow-white spots. *Pupa* up to 22 mm. Buff with golden mirror-like panels. Hangs head-down from a leaf. **VARIATION** Sexes similar, but ♂ has grey sex mark at anal angle of hind wing. **SIMILAR SPECIES** Chief (p. 22) has ochreous, not white, forewing spots. Mimics include ♀ Mocker Swallowtail form *cenea* (p. 127). **STATUS** Common and widespread.

J F M A M J J A S O N D

**NYMPHALIDAE:** DANAINAE / MONARCHS, FRIARS, EVENING BROWNS

## Chief
**Toordokter**
*Amauris echeria echeria*      55–70 mm

**HABITS** Slow, lazy, usually high flight. Descends to feed from flowers. Males swarm on damaged or wilted plants to imbibe alkaloids. **HABITAT** Forest. **EARLY STAGES** *Egg* a faintly ribbed oval. Cream-white. Laid singly or in a small cluster under a leaf of a *Cynanchum*, *Tylophora* or another of the forest Apocynaceae. *Larva* up to 38 mm. Greyish-black with rows of yellow and white spots; has black filaments like those of an African Monarch larva. *Pupa* up to 22 mm. Buff with silver-gold mirror-like panels. Hangs head-down from a leaf. **VARIATION** Sexes similar, but ♂ has grey sex mark at anal angle of hind wing. **SIMILAR SPECIES** Layman (p. 21) has white forewing spots. Palpi carry a white spot, not a line. Mimics include False Chief (p. 58). **STATUS** Widespread but scarce.

J F M A M J J A S O N D

## Twilight Brown
**Skemer-bruintjie**
*Melanitis leda*      58–72 mm

**HABITS** Shade-loving. Seldom flies by day, unless disturbed from forest floor. Active at dusk. **HABITAT** Forest and savanna. Penetrates arid areas along rivers. **EARLY STAGES** *Egg* oval. Yellow-white. Laid individually on a blade of grass, usually *Oplismenus hirtellus*, *Setaria megaphylla*, or another food grass. *Larva* up to 50 mm. Spindle-shaped with forked tail and horned head. Green with variable pattern of green and black. *Pupa* up to 20 mm. Green with humped back. Hangs head-down from a leaf. **VARIATION** Sexes similar, but ♂ smaller. Dry season form (middle image) has much larger eyespots. **SIMILAR SPECIES** Yellow-banded Evening Brown (p. 23) lacks eyespots and has prominent yellow forewing bands. **STATUS** Common and widespread.

J F M A M J J A S O N D

## Yellow-banded Evening Brown
**Geelband-skemerbruintjie**
*Gnophodes betsimena diversa*     **55–70 mm**

**HABITS** Shade-loving. Seldom flies during the day, unless disturbed from forest floor. Active at dusk. **HABITAT** Undergrowth in dense riverine forest within the valleys in its range. **EARLY STAGES** *Egg* spherical with truncated base. Pale yellow-green. Laid singly on a blade of *Setaria megaphylla* or another forest grass. *Larva* up to 52 mm. Forked tail and blunt-topped head. Green with pale stripes. *Pupa* up to 20 mm. Waxy yellow-green. Hangs head-down from a leaf. **VARIATION** Sexes similar, but ♂ slightly smaller. Wet season form not found in SA. **SIMILAR SPECIES** Twilight Brown (p. 22) has eyespots and lacks yellow forewing bands. **STATUS** Rare.

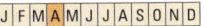

## Common Bush Brown
**Swart-bosbruintjie**
*Bicyclus safitza safitza*     **40–48 mm**

**HABITS** Slow bobbing flight among low vegetation on forest floor. Fond of rotten fruit. **HABITAT** Forest and heavily wooded areas in savanna. **EARLY STAGES** *Egg* spherical. Transparent yellow-green. Laid singly on a blade of *Oplismenus hirtellus*. *Larva* up to 33 mm. Tapers towards tail. Two blunt head horns. Dull yellow with diagonal brown stripes and a dark dorsal line. *Pupa* up to 15 mm. Green to brown with contrasting markings. Hangs head-down from a leaf. **VARIATION** ♂ slightly smaller and darker than ♀. Wet season form (not shown) has greatly enlarged ocelli. **SIMILAR SPECIES** Squinting Bush Brown (p. 24) dry season form has off-centre pupil in underside forewing ocellus; in ♂ outer hair pencil on upper side hind wing is pale fuscous brown, not black. **STATUS** Common and widespread.

## NYMPHALIDAE: SATYRINAE / BUSH BROWNS

### Squinting Bush Brown
Skeeloog-bosbruintjie
*Bicyclus anynana anynana*      35–45 mm

**HABITS** Slow bobbing flight among low vegetation on forest floor. Fond of rotten fruit. **HABITAT** Wooded savanna and forest, especially along the coast. **EARLY STAGES** *Egg* spherical. Transparent yellow-green. Laid singly on a blade of *Oplismenus hirtellus*. *Larva* up to 28 mm. Tapers towards tail. Two short head horns. Dull yellow with diagonal brown stripes and dark dorsal line. *Pupa* up to 12 mm. Green to brown with contrasting markings. Hangs head-down from a leaf. **VARIATION** ♂ slightly smaller and darker than ♀. Wet season form (bottom image) has greatly enlarged ocelli. **SIMILAR SPECIES** Common Bush Brown (p. 23) dry season form has centred pupil in underside forewing ocellus and the ♂ has fuscous black outer hair pencil on upper side hind wing. **STATUS** Widespread but scarce.

J F **M A M J J A S O** N D

### Grizzled Bush Brown
Spikkel-bosbruintjie
*Bicyclus ena*      38–48 mm

**HABITS** Low, bobbing flight in the shade of thick vegetation. **HABITAT** Wooded savanna. **EARLY STAGES** *Egg* spherical. Transparent white. Laid singly on a blade of *Pennisetum clandestinum*. *Larva* up to 33 mm. Tapers towards tail. Head has two short horns. Body green with darker diagonal stripes and dorsal line. *Pupa* up to 15 mm. Green to brown with contrasting markings. Hangs head-down from a leaf. **VARIATION** Sexes similar, but ♂ slightly smaller. Wet season form (not shown) darker. **SIMILAR SPECIES** Other bush brown dry season forms have much larger ocelli. ♂ Grizzled Bush Brown's upper side hind wing hair pencils are jet black, never brown. **STATUS** Scarce and local.

J F M **A M J J A S O** N D

NYMPHALIDAE: SATYRINAE / BUSH BROWNS, BEAUTIES

## Eyed Bush Brown
**Moeraswagter**
*Heteropsis perspicua perspicua*     **38–48 mm**

**HABITS** Low bobbing flight among long grass. Settles with wings opening and closing. **HABITAT** Wetlands, riversides and dams. **EARLY STAGES** *Egg* spherical with flattened base. Transparent white. Laid singly on a blade of the grass *Panicum maximum*. *Larva* up to 30 mm. Tapers towards tail. Two short head horns. Body pale salmon pink with greenish diagonal stripes and dorsal line. *Pupa* up to 12 mm. Green to brown with contrasting markings. Hangs head-down from a leaf. **VARIATION** Sexes similar, but ♂ slightly smaller. Upper side slightly darker in dry season form (not shown) with less prominent orange ring around forewing ocellus. Centre of underside forewing ocellus in dry season form is pure white with no black. **SIMILAR SPECIES** None. **STATUS** Widespread but scarce.

J F M A M J J A S O N D

## Table Mountain Beauty
**Bergnooientjie**
*Aeropetes tulbaghia*     **70–90 mm**

**HABITS** Fast flapping flight at medium height. Settles often on flowers, particularly red or orange species. Rests in the shade of large rocks. **HABITAT** High mountain grassland and fynbos. **EARLY STAGES** *Egg* an elongated dome. Transparent white. Scattered among grasses like *Stenotaphrum secundatum*. Reared in captivity on other grasses like *Pennisetum clandestinum*. *Larva* up to 65 mm. Body varies from pale yellow-green to red-brown. Head brown. Lives at the base of a grass clump. *Pupa* up to 50 mm. Dull pale yellow with black markings. Hangs head-down from a leaf or stem. **VARIATION** Sexes similar, but ♂ smaller. **SIMILAR SPECIES** None. **STATUS** Locally common.

J F M A M J J A S O N D

## Forest Beauty
Bosprag
*Paralethe dendrophilus*  45–70 mm

**HABITS** Flapping flight; skulks in shade. Rests on tree bark. Attracted to rotting fruit. **HABITAT** Afrotemperate forest. **EARLY STAGES** *Egg* almost spherical. Transparent white, turning pale brown. Scattered among *Panicum deustum* grass; reared in captivity on grasses like *Ehrharta erecta*. *Larva* up to 40 mm. Stout with forked tail. Reddish buff-brown with darker diamond pattern dorsally and diagonal lateral stripes. *Pupa* up to 25 mm. Rounded. Brick red. Hangs head-down from a leaf. **VARIATION** Sexes similar. Forewing markings are large and white in northern subspecies *junodi* (not shown), smaller in *indosa* and *albina*, and suffused with more orange in more southerly specimens, but fully orange in nominate. **SIMILAR SPECIES** None. **STATUS** Locally common.

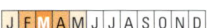

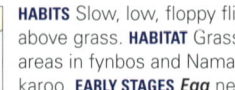

## Cape Autumn Widow
Kaapse-herfsweduwee
*Dira clytus*  45–55 mm

**HABITS** Slow, low, floppy flight above grass. **HABITAT** Grassy areas in fynbos and Nama karoo. **EARLY STAGES** *Egg* nearly spherical. Transparent white, turning pale brown. Scattered in *Panicum deustum* grass. Reared in captivity on grasses like *Ehrharta erecta*. *Larva* up to 32 mm. Stout with forked tail. Pale buff with black dorsal pattern and diagonal lateral stripes. *Pupa* up to 12 mm. Rounded. Brown with black speckling and stripes. Forms in leaf litter. **VARIATION** Sexes similar, but ♀ smaller. Subspecies *eurina* (E. Cape) larger and paler than nominate subspecies. **SIMILAR SPECIES** Spring Widow (W. and N. Cape) has distinct geometric pattern on underside hind wing. Pondoland Widow (p. 27) is much larger. **STATUS** Common and widespread.

NYMPHALIDAE: SATYRINAE / WIDOWS

## Pondoland Widow
Pondoland-weduwee
*Dira oxylus*   50–65 mm

**HABITS** Colonies may be huge. Slow flapping flight just above the grass. **HABITAT** Grassy slopes. **EARLY STAGES** *Egg* nearly spherical. Transparent white, turning pale brown. Scattered on food grass, probably *Merxmuellera stricta*; reared in captivity on grasses like *Ehrharta erecta*. *Larva* up to 24 mm. Very stout with forked tail. Pale buff, almost entirely obscured by black markings. *Pupa* up to 13 mm. Rounded. Dark fuscous brown with few markings. Forms in leaf litter. **VARIATION** Sexes similar, but ♀ smaller. **SIMILAR SPECIES** Cape Autumn Widow (p. 26) much smaller with more apical spots on forewing. Swanepoel's and Janse's widows (Lim. mountains) very similar, but separated from Pondoland Widow on distribution. **STATUS** Locally common.

J F M A M J J A S O N D

## Dingaan's Widow
Dingaan-se-weduwee
*Dingana dingana*   52–55 mm

**HABITS** Slow flapping flight around large rocks. Settles frequently on flowers. **HABITAT** Rocky, grassy slopes. **EARLY STAGES** Details not recorded. Likely to be similar in many respects to Wolkberg Widow *Dingana clara*, whose details follow here. *Egg* almost spherical. Pale yellow, turning pale brown. Scattered on grass; reared in captivity on *Ehrharta erecta*. *Larva* up to 30 mm. Very stout with forked tail. Dark brown, almost entirely obscured by black markings. Shelters at the base of a grass clump. *Pupa* up to 17 mm. Rounded. Colour not recorded. Forms in a clump of grass. **VARIATION** Sexes similar, but ♀ smaller. **SIMILAR SPECIES** Six other *Dingana* widows separated on distribution. **STATUS** Threatened.

J F M A M J J A S O N D

## Clark's Widow
Clark-se-weduwee
*Serradinga clarki*      45–52 mm

**HABITS** Slow sailing flight over steep mountain slopes. Settles often on flowers. **HABITAT** Alpine Drakensberg grassland. **EARLY STAGES Egg** domed. Pale yellow, turning pale brown. Scattered in *Merxmuellera* grasses. Reared in captivity on *Pennisetum clandestinum*. **Larva** size not recorded. Spindle-shaped. Dark fuscous brown with black markings and paler diagonal lateral markings. **Pupa** details not recorded, but resembles pupa of a *Dingana*. **VARIATION** Sexes similar, but ♀ smaller with orange-tinged white upper side forewing marks. Four geographically distinct subspecies. **SIMILAR SPECIES** Bowker's Widow (E. Cape, KZN, Les.) larger, darker and occurs at higher altitude than Clark's. Kammanassie Widow (restricted to that mountain range) is darker with more angular hind wing shape. **STATUS** Locally common.

J F M A M J J A S O N D

## Mintha Widow
Mintha-weduwee
*Torynesis mintha*      40–48 mm

**HABITS** Flutters low among food grasses. Reluctant to settle, except for the ♀ when she lays eggs. **HABITAT** Food grasses in fynbos. **EARLY STAGES Egg** domed. Pale yellow, turning pinkish-brown. Loosely scattered on *Merxmuellera stricta* or a *Ficinia* restio. **Larva** up to 30 mm. Spindle-shaped. Buff-brown with longitudinal brown dorsal and lateral stripes. Lacks diagonal lateral markings seen on other widow larvae. **Pupa** up to 13 mm. Rounded. Reddish-brown. Forms among grass roots. **VARIATION** Sexes similar, but ♀ smaller and more colourful. Subspecies *piquetbergensis* (Piketberg, Moorreesburg, W. Cape) (not shown) has less prominent pattern on underside hind wing. **SIMILAR SPECIES** Four similar *Torynesis* widows (Namaqualand to Les.) are separated on distribution. **STATUS** Locally common.

J F M A M J J A S O N D

NYMPHALIDAE: SATYRINAE / WIDOWS, SHADEFLIES

## Spring Widow
**Lente-weduwee**
*Tarsocera cassus*             42–57 mm

**HABITS** Wandering flight, but fast if disturbed. Settles often on flowers or the ground. **HABITAT** Rocky slopes and hill summits in fynbos and Nama karoo. **EARLY STAGES** *Egg* domed. Pale yellow, turning golden brown. Scattered loosely among grasses; reared in captivity on *Hyparrhenia hirta* and *Lolium temulentum*. *Larva* size not recorded. Sandy brown with darker longitudinal dorsal and lateral stripes and paler brown diagonal lateral markings. *Pupa* size not recorded. Sandy brown with fuscous brown speckling and wing case veins. Forms among grass roots. **VARIATION** Sexes similar. Subspecies *outeniqua* (eastern W. Cape) (not shown) has dark patch before upper side forewing eyespot. **SIMILAR SPECIES** Six of the *Tarsocera* widows look similar (Namaqualand to E. Cape); told apart by genitalic dissection. **STATUS** Locally common.

## Zulu Shadefly
**Zoeloeskadu-bruintjie**
*Coenyra hebe*             32–38 mm

**HABITS** Flies low among grass and bushes or on forest margins. Favours shade, hence its common name. **HABITAT** Wooded savanna and thick bush. **EARLY STAGES** *Egg* a flattened dome. White, developing pinkish-red stripes. Laid on stems of unknown wild grass; reared in captivity on *Ehrharta erecta*. *Larva* up to 28 mm. Brownish-green with reddish longitudinal dorsal and lateral stripes. Head pale yellow-orange. *Pupa* up to 15 mm. Colour not recorded. Attached to a silken pad on a stem or leaf. **VARIATION** Sexes similar. **SIMILAR SPECIES** Pondo Shadefly (KZN) has wider, pale orange underside bands. Secucuni Shadefly (northern E. Cape) has narrower red bands. Natal Brown (bushveld, northeastern SA) has fewer underside bands. **STATUS** Locally common.

NYMPHALIDAE: SATYRINAE / SHADEFLIES, BROWNS

## Dark-webbed Ringlet
Gestreepte-ringetjie
*Physcaeneura panda*        34–49 mm

**HABITS** Flies low over grass. Settles often on the ground or on flowers. **HABITAT** Savanna and bushveld. **EARLY STAGES** *Egg* domed. Transparent yellow, developing brick-red spots. Laid singly on stems and leaves of unknown food grasses. Reared in captivity on *Ehrharta erecta* and *Pennisetum clandestinum*. *Larva* up to 20 mm. Whitish with longitudinal, dull purple dorsal and lateral stripes. *Pupa* up to 14 mm. Light green. Attached to a silken pad on a stem or leaf. **VARIATION** Sexes similar. **SIMILAR SPECIES** Shadeflies and other ringlets are similar in appearance and habits, but Dark-webbed Ringlet's underside is unique. Note that Dark-webbed Ringlet is more closely related to the shadeflies than the *Ypthima* species that are also called ringlets. **STATUS** Locally common.

J F M A M J J A S O N D

## Rainforest Brown
Reënwoud-bosbruintjie
*Cassionympha cassius*        34–42 mm

**HABITS** Flies low along forest margins and pathways. Settles often, opening and closing wings jerkily. **HABITAT** Coastal forest and thick bush. **EARLY STAGES** *Egg* domed. Pale yellow, developing brown spots. Laid singly on a blade of the grasses *Juncus capensis* or *Pentaschistis capensis*. *Larva* up to 23 mm. Spindle-shaped with forked tail. Dull pale green, reddish-brown or greenish-brown. *Pupa* up to 14 mm. Green, or green and black. Suspended head-down from a stem or leaf. **VARIATION** Sexes similar. **SIMILAR SPECIES** Cape (W., N. and E. Cape) and Camdeboo (E. Cape) browns are similar in size and shape, but neither has dark brown underside bands. **STATUS** Common and widespread.

J F M A M J J A S O N D

NYMPHALIDAE: SATYRINAE / BROWNS

## Boland Brown
Boland-bruintjie
*Melampias huebneri*      **33–38 mm**

**HABITS** Sustained fluttering flight on grassy hillsides. Swarms after good winter rains. **HABITAT** Coastal fynbos, Nama and succulent karoo. **EARLY STAGES** *Egg* domed. Transparent white, developing reddish bands. Laid singly on a blade of an unknown food grass. Reared in captivity on *Avena sativa* and *Ehrharta erecta*. *Larva* up to 23 mm. Dull green with darker, white-edged longitudinal stripes. *Pupa* up to 14 mm. Pale green edged with pale pink. Suspended head-down from a stem or leaf. **VARIATION** Sexes similar. Subspecies *steniptera* (Namaqualand) (not shown) has elongated pointed forewings. **SIMILAR SPECIES** Resembles many small *Pseudonympha* and *Stygionympha* browns, but distinguished by dark underside with tiny white spots. **STATUS** Common and widespread.

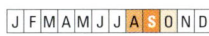

---

## Neita Brown
Neita-bruintjie
*Neita neita*      **45–58 mm**

**HABITS** Sustained fluttering flight on grassy hillsides. Often settles on flowers. May shelter in the shade of large bushes. **HABITAT** Grassland and grassy savanna. **EARLY STAGES** Details not recorded, but larva likely to feed on grass. **VARIATION** Sexes similar. Size of eyespots varies greatly between populations. **SIMILAR SPECIES** Loteni (KZN) and D'Urban's (E. Cape) browns are very similar, but smaller with fewer eyespots. D'Urban's has tiny eyespots and distinctive dark bands on underside hind wing. **STATUS** Locally common.

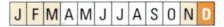

NYMPHALIDAE: SATYRINAE / BROWNS

## Natal Brown
**Natalse-bruintjie**
*Coenyropsis natalii*     34–38 mm

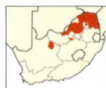

**HABITS** Flies low among grass near bushes and along forest margins. Like a shadefly, is fond of shaded vegetation under large bushes. **HABITAT** Grassland and grassy savanna. **EARLY STAGES** Details not recorded, but larva likely to feed on grass. **VARIATION** Sexes similar. Subspecies *poetuloides* (Wolkberg) (not shown) has larger apical eyespots on upper side forewing. **SIMILAR SPECIES** Shadeflies similar in habits and appearance but with brighter patterns on underside hind wing. Savanna Brown (NW, Lim., Mpu.) very similar but larger with more orange surrounding apical eyespot in underside forewing. **STATUS** Widespread but scarce.

J F M A M J J A S O N D

## Drakensberg Brown
**Drakensberg-bruintjie**
*Pseudonympha poetula*     42–46 mm

**HABITS** Low, rapid, sustained flight on mountainsides. Flies very early in the season and is usually among the first butterflies seen in spring. **HABITAT** Montane grassland. **EARLY STAGES** Details not recorded, but larva likely to feed on grass. **VARIATION** Sexes similar. **SIMILAR SPECIES** Superficially resembles Trimen's (p. 33), Gaika (Les., KZN, E. Cape) and Golden Gate (FS) browns, but underside hind wing markings are distinguishing. **STATUS** Locally common.

J F M A M J J A S O N D

**NYMPHALIDAE:** SATYRINAE / BROWNS

## Trimen's Brown
Trimen-se-bruintjie
*Pseudonympha trimenii* **40–56 mm**

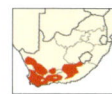

**HABITS** Low, bouncing, fluttering flight among clumps of its food plant. **HABITAT** Grassy patches in mountainous fynbos, Nama and succulent karoo vegetation. **EARLY STAGES** *Egg* large with rounded ends. Pale green, developing reddish bands. Laid singly on a blade of the grass *Merxmuellera stricta*. *Larva* up to 26 mm. Spindle-shaped with flat tail. Pale green with darker green, white-edged longitudinal stripes. *Pupa* up to 15 mm. Green edged with black. Hangs head-down from its tail. **VARIATION** Sexes similar. Four very similar subspecies occur across the range, among them *P. t. namaquana* shown here. **SIMILAR SPECIES** Gaika (Les., KZN, E. Cape) and Golden Gate (FS) browns more brightly coloured with larger orange-russet patches on all wings. **STATUS** Locally common.

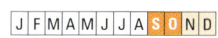

J F M A M J J A **S O N** D

## Silver-bottom Brown
Tower-bruintjie
*Pseudonympha magus* **40–44 mm**

**HABITS** Low bobbing flight. **HABITAT** Grassy areas in fynbos and karoo vegetation. **EARLY STAGES** *Egg* large with rounded ends. Transparent green-white, turning yellow with reddish bands. Laid singly on unknown grasses; reared in captivity on *Ehrharta erecta* and *Cynodon dactylon*. *Larva* up to 24 mm. Spindle-shaped with forked tail. Yellow-green with faint darker green longitudinal stripes. *Pupa* size not recorded. Yellow-green, edged with black; has blue-green dorsal line. Hangs head-down from tail in leaf debris. **VARIATION** Sexes similar, but ♀ has more rounded wings. **SIMILAR SPECIES** False Silver-bottom (E. Cape, Les., KZN, Mpu., FS, Gau., Lim.), Swanepoel's (FS, Mpu., Lim.) and Vári's (W. and E. Cape, KZN, Mpu., Les., Lim.) browns are larger, brighter with more conspicuous underside silver. **STATUS** Common and widespread.

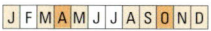

J F M A M J J A S **O** N D

**NYMPHALIDAE:** SATYRINAE / BROWNS

## Spotted-eye Brown
Koloog-bruintjie
*Paternympha narycia*     40–47 mm

**HABITS** Weak flight, close to the ground. Frequently settles on rocks. **HABITAT** Grassland and grassy savanna. **EARLY STAGES** Details not recorded. **VARIATION** Sexes similar, but ♀ has more rounded wings. **SIMILAR SPECIES** Big-eye Brown (Waterberg to Dullstroom) is very similar, but apical eyespot on upper side forewing is far larger and contains more white spots. **STATUS** Locally common.

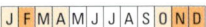

## Western Hillside Brown
Westelike-rantbruintjie
*Stygionympha vigilans*     45–48 mm

**HABITS** Rapid, jerky flight among rocks on steep slopes. Very alert. **HABITAT** Grassy areas on rocky ridges from sea level to high altitude. **EARLY STAGES** *Egg* finely ribbed and nearly spherical. Milk white, turning pale brown with a thin brown band. Laid singly on a blade of the grass *Ischyrolepis cincinnata*; reared in captivity on *Ehrharta erecta*. *Larva* up to 32 mm. Spindle-shaped with forked tail. Yellow-green with faint brown longitudinal stripes. *Pupa* details not recorded. **VARIATION** Sexes similar, but ♀ has more rounded wings. **SIMILAR SPECIES** Eastern Hillside Brown (E. Cape, Les., FS, KZN, Mpu., Lim., Swa.) has larger russet patches on upper side forewing and, unlike most Western Hillside Browns, never has eyespot at anal angle of underside hind wing. **STATUS** Locally common.

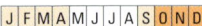

## Wichgraf's Hillside Brown

Wichgraf-se-rantbruintjie
*Stygionympha wichgrafi*         **40–50 mm**

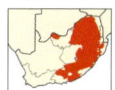

**HABITS** Fast jerky flight. Alert. **HABITAT** Montane grassland. **EARLY STAGES** *Egg* ribbed, nearly spherical. White, developing thin brown band. Laid singly and raised in captivity on unknown grasses. *Larva* up to 30 mm. Spindle-shaped. Tail forked. Red-brown above, yellow-green below with thin white stripes. *Pupa* details not recorded. **VARIATION** Sexes similar, but ♀ has more rounded wings. Three subspecies, including *williami* shown here. **SIMILAR SPECIES** Eastern (E. Cape to Lim.) and Western (p. 34) hillside browns larger and lack eyespot in underside hind wing area M1. Robertson's, Van Son's and Gerald's hillside browns (E. to N. Cape) darker. Karoo Hillside Brown (W. Cape to FS) smaller, darker with buff spots under hind wing. In Curle's Hillside Brown (KZN to Mpu.) ochre upper side forewing spot doesn't reach ocellus. **STATUS** Common and widespread.

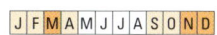

---

## Impure Ringlet

Vuil-ringetjie
*Ypthima impura paupera*         **32–38 cm**

**HABITS** Rapid jerky flight just above grass level. **HABITAT** Grass in moist savanna. **EARLY STAGES** *Egg* a smooth sphere. Cream-white, developing thin brown band. Laid singly on unknown grass; raised in captivity on *Ehrharta erecta*. *Larva* up to 25 mm. Spindle-shaped with forked tail. Pinkish-white with faint brown longitudinal stripes. *Pupa* up to 12 mm. Pinkish-white. Hangs head-down from a silk pad fixed to a leaf, twig or debris. **VARIATION** Sexes similar, but ♀ has more rounded wings. **SIMILAR SPECIES** Four other species of *Ypthima* ringlets occur in SA. African Ringlet (p. 36) is most common and has single (not double) marginal line on upper side hind wing. **STATUS** Scarce and local.

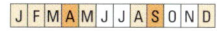

## African Ringlet
Afrikaanse-ringetjie
*Ypthima asterope*          30–38 mm

**HABITS** Rapid jerky flight just above grass level. **HABITAT** Grassy areas in dry savanna, Nama and succulent karoo. **EARLY STAGES** Surprisingly for such a widespread insect, its life history is not yet described. **VARIATION** Sexes similar, but ♀ has more rounded wings. Two similar subspecies, nominate in the east and *hereroica* (not shown) in the west. **SIMILAR SPECIES** Four other species of *Ypthima* ringlets occur in SA. Impure Ringlet (p. 35) has double marginal line on upper side hind wing. Condamin's (Lim.) and Clubbed (Lim.) ringlets are rare and almost identical to African Ringlet. Granular Ringlet (a few locations in Zululand and Mpumalanga) has extended grey patch around upper side forewing eyespot. **STATUS** Common and widespread.

## Wanderer
Swartbont-rooitjie
*Acraea aganice aganice*        60–75 mm

**HABITS** Slow floating flight. Remains in, or just below, forest canopy. **HABITAT** Lowland and riverine forest. **EARLY STAGES** *Egg* a finely ribbed cross-braced oval. Cream-white. Laid in large batches on Passifloraceae such as *Adenia gummifera* or *Basananthe zanzibarica*. *Larva* up to 38 mm. Cylindrical. Pale green with long branched spines. Gregarious. *Pupa* up to 30 mm. Pale green-white with four pairs of long red spines along abdomen. **VARIATION** ♂ pale yellow. ♀ has white markings. **SIMILAR SPECIES** Dusky Acraea (p. 42) is smaller and lacks pale spot below upper side forewing apical band. The False Wanderer (p. 57) mimics it, but has dark-edged spots at base of upper side hind wing and upper side forewing. **STATUS** Common and widespread.

NYMPHALIDAE: HELICONIINAE / BITTER ACRAEAS

## Garden Acraea
Tuin-rooitjie
*Acraea horta*      45–53 mm

**HABITS** Slow floating flight a few metres high, close to food plants. **HABITAT** Afrotemperate forest as well as gardens with food plants. **EARLY STAGES** *Egg* a finely ribbed and cross-braced oval. Cream-white, turning red then brown. Laid in large batches on *Kiggelaria africana*. *Larva* up to 34 mm. Cylindrical. Blue-black above and cream below with branched spines. Gregarious. *Pupa* up to 19 mm. Orange-yellow with black markings. Suspended head-down from a silk pad. **VARIATION** ♂ brick red. ♀ dirty buff. **SIMILAR SPECIES** Many *Acraea* are red with black spots. Closest in appearance is the Wandering Donkey Acraea (N. Cape, NW, FS, Gau., Lim., Mpu., KZN, E. Cape and Swa.), but it is pinker with sparser markings, and the marginal band on its upper side hind wing has pale spots surrounded by black. **STATUS** Common and widespread.

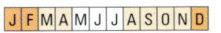

## Clear-wing Acraea
Glasvlerk-rooitjie
*Acraea rabbaiae perlucida*      45–65 mm

**HABITS** Slow dancing flight in canopy, occasionally settling low down. Sometimes roosts *en masse*. **HABITAT** Lowveld forest and savanna. **EARLY STAGES** *Egg* elongated with faint cross-ribbing. Cream-white, turning grey. Laid in large batches on leaves of *Basananthe zanzibarica*. *Larva* size not recorded. Cylindrical with long branched spines. Reddish-brown with first three and final segments dull yellow. Gregarious. *Pupa* size not recorded. Elongated. Cream with fine black lines. Orange-centred black-ringed spots on abdomen. Attached by the tail to a leaf or twig. **VARIATION** ♀ larger. **SIMILAR SPECIES** None. **STATUS** Rare.

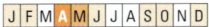

## NYMPHALIDAE: HELICONIINAE / BITTER ACRAEAS

♂

### Rainforest Acraea
Reënwoud-rooitjie
*Acraea boopis boopis*  **45–58 mm**

**HABITS** ♂ flies slowly, high up in the canopy, occasionally settling low down to accost a ♀. Both sexes fond of flowers and mud puddles. **HABITAT** Lowland and escarpment forest. **EARLY STAGES** Details not recorded. Larva feeds on *Lauridia tetragona*, *Maytenus acuminata* and *Rawsonia lucida*. **VARIATION** ♂ deep red; ♀ has dark buff ground colour. **SIMILAR SPECIES** East Coast Acraea (KZN) has similar markings, but is much larger and the ♀ is white whereas ♀ Rainforest Acraea is buff. **STATUS** Locally common.

♀

♀

♂

### Fiery Acraea
Vuur-rooitjie
*Acraea acrita acrita*  **45–55 mm**

**HABITS** Rapid fluttering flight across open ground on margins of bushy habitat. Settles on shrubs at head height. **HABITAT** Wooded savanna and sand forest. **EARLY STAGES** Details not recorded, but further north larva is known to feed on *Adenia* in the Passifloraceae. **VARIATION** ♂ fiery orange and red. ♀ suffused with black. Wet season forms (not shown) of both sexes have much more black. **SIMILAR SPECIES** Natal Acraea (p. 39) has similar markings but far duller colours and upper side forewing veins are picked out in black. **STATUS** Scarce and local.

♂

♀

NYMPHALIDAE: HELICONIINAE / BITTER ACRAEAS

## Natal Acraea
Natal-rooitjie
*Acraea natalica natalica* **55–65 mm**

**HABITS** Slow random flight across open ground on margins of bushy habitat. Settles often on flowers. **HABITAT** Savanna, forest and urban areas. **EARLY STAGES** *Egg* domed with cross-ribbing. Cream-white, turning salmon. Laid in clusters on an *Adenia*. *Larva* up to 36 mm. Cylindrical with branched spines. Underside cream; upper side yellow with black longitudinal stripes. *Pupa* up to 24 mm. Slender. Cream-white. Black lines on abdomen enclose yellow spots. Black veins on wing cases. Attached by the tail to a leaf or twig. **VARIATION** ♀ darker with more yellow than ♂. Dry season forms (not shown) have less black. **SIMILAR SPECIES** Fiery Acraea (p. 38) much brighter with no black on veins. Black-tipped Acraea (below) smaller and pinker with distinctive black upper side forewing tips. **STATUS** Common and widespread.

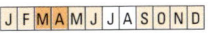

## Black-tipped Acraea
Swartpunt-rooitjie
*Acraea caldarena caldarena* **40–55 mm**

**HABITS** Slow flight close to the ground. Settles often on low vegetation or flowers. **HABITAT** Dry savanna. **EARLY STAGES** *Egg* oval with cross-ribbing. Cream-white, turning pale dull yellow. Laid singly or in small clusters on *Tricliceras longipedunculatum*. *Larva* up to 32 mm. Cylindrical. Pale brown with branched black spines. *Pupa* up to 22 mm. Slender. Wing cases drab white with black lines. Abdomen cream with orange spots outlined in black. Attached by the tail to a leaf or twig. **VARIATION** Sexes similar. Wet season form (not shown) tends to be darker. **SIMILAR SPECIES** Natal Acraea (above) large and more heavily marked. Little (NW, N. Cape, Lim., Gau., Mpu., KZN and Swa) and Clear-spotted (NW, Lim., Gau., Mpu., KZN and Swa.) acraeas may have similar colouring, but lack black upper side forewing tips. **STATUS** Scarce but widespread.

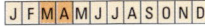

# NYMPHALIDAE: HELICONIINAE / BITTER ACRAEAS

## Window Acraea
**Rooibokkie-rooitjie**
*Acraea oncaea*  **40–55 mm**

**HABITS** Slow flight near the ground. Settles on low vegetation or flowers. **HABITAT** Coastal and inland savanna. **EARLY STAGES** *Egg* oval with cross-ribbing. Cream-white, turning pale chocolate brown. Laid in clusters on *Xylotheca kraussiana*, *Tricliceras longipedunculatum* or an *Adenia*. *Larva* up to 32 mm. Cylindrical. Salmon with branched black spines. May have black transverse lines. *Pupa* up to 22 mm. Elongated. Pale salmon with black lines on wing veins and black-ringed orange spots on abdomen. Attached by the tail to a leaf or twig. **VARIATION** ♀ varies from tawny orange to grey-black and is darker than ♂ with prominent white apical patches on upper side forewing. **SIMILAR SPECIES** Several of the *Acraea* have black spots on orange-pink ground, but lack black upper side forewing interneural lines. **STATUS** Locally common.

| J | F | M | A | M | J | J | A | S | O | N | D |

## Acara Acraea
**Acara-rooitjie**
*Acraea acara acara*  **55–72 mm**

**HABITS** Slow sustained flight through the bush; rapid if molested. Settles on leaves of trees. **HABITAT** Forest and savanna. **EARLY STAGES** *Egg* an elongated barrel with cross-ribbing. Yellow. Laid in clusters on *Adenia glauca*. *Larva* up to 35 mm. Cylindrical. Salmon with black branched spines; sometimes has black transverse lines. *Pupa* up to 24 mm. Slender. White to yellow or orange with black lines on wing veins and black-ringed orange spots on abdomen. Attached by the tail to a leaf or twig. **VARIATION** ♀ much darker than ♂ with no fiery red or orange. **SIMILAR SPECIES** Trimen's and Barber's acraeas (both further west, in more arid savanna) are unicoloured – orange and red respectively. **STATUS** Scarce but widespread.

| J | F | M | A | M | J | J | A | S | O | N | D |

NYMPHALIDAE: HELICONIINAE / BITTER ACRAEAS

## Broad-bordered Acraea
Kersboom-rooitjie
*Acraea anemosa*                           **50–64 mm**

**HABITS** Slow sustained flight through the bush, but rapid if molested. Settles on leaves. **HABITAT** Forest and savanna. **EARLY STAGES Egg** details not fully recorded; known to be yellowish-cream. Laid in clusters on *Adenia glauca*, *A. digitata* or *A. venenata*. **Larva** size not recorded. Red-brown with black branched spines; the first four and last two spines are yellow. **Pupa** size not recorded. Dingy white with black lines on wing veins and black-ringed orange spots on abdomen. Attached by the tail to a leaf or twig. **VARIATION** Sexes similar, but ♀ usually darker. Some individuals have reddish upper side hind wing or, more rarely, a large white patch. **SIMILAR SPECIES** None. **STATUS** Scarce but widespread.

J F M A M J J A S O N D

## Blood-red Acraea
Bloed-rooitjie
*Acraea petraea*                           **45–55 mm**

**HABITS** Slow flight, 1–3 m high, near to food plants. ♂ territorial. **HABITAT** Coastal and escarpment forest. **EARLY STAGES Egg** a cross-ribbed barrel. Translucent yellow, turning yellow-brown. Laid in clusters on *Xylotheca kraussiana*. **Larva** up to 30 mm. Cylindrical. Variable, but usually cream below and yellow above, marked with black transverse and longitudinal lines and covered in blue-black branched spines. **Pupa** up to 20 mm. Variable, white to yellow or deep orange, usually with black lines on wing veins and black-ringed orange spots on abdomen. Attached by the tail to a substrate. **VARIATION** ♂ ground colour always red; ♀ red to brown with prominent white apical patch on upper side forewing. **SIMILAR SPECIES** ♂ unmistakable. Some ♀ forms resemble ♀ Window Acraea (p. 40). **STATUS** Locally common.

J F M A M J J A S O N D

## NYMPHALIDAE: HELICONIINAE / BITTER ACRAEAS

### Dusky-veined Acraea
**Vuilvenster-rooitjie**
*Telchinia igola*      **40–53 mm**

**HABITS** Slow hovering flight in canopy. Often also seen lower down, on flowers or near food plants. **HABITAT** Lowland, coastal and escarpment forest. **EARLY STAGES** *Egg* cylindrical with cross-ribbing. Yellow, turning salmon. Laid in multilayered clusters on *Urera trinervis*. *Larva* up to 30 mm. Dull yellow-green with transverse bands of black branched spines. Gregarious. *Pupa* up to 17 mm. Cream with black and yellow spots. Wing veins outlined in black. Attached by the tail to a leaf or twig. **VARIATION** ♂ always deep red, but ♀ may be brick red or yellowish-cream. **SIMILAR SPECIES** Rainforest Acraea (p. 38) similar, but has blockier black markings and ♀ is never pale cream. **STATUS** Locally common.

### Dusky Acraea
**Boerbok-rooitjie**
*Telchinia esebria*      **45–60 mm**

**HABITS** Slow flight along forest edges and pathways. Settles frequently. Fond of flowers. **HABITAT** Lowland, coastal and escarpment forest. **EARLY STAGES** *Egg* cylindrical with cross-ribbing. Pale yellow. Laid in clusters on the leaves of a *Urera, Laportea, Pouzolzia, Obetia* or other nettle species. *Larva* up to 35 mm. Dull yellow-green with bands of black branched spines. Gregarious. *Pupa* up to 18 mm. Cream with black-edged yellow spots. Wing veins outlined in black. Attached by the tail to a leaf or twig. **VARIATION** Several forms. Pale markings may be all cream (form *protea*), all white (form *monteironis*) or ochre red with white bands on forewing tip (form *esebria*). **SIMILAR SPECIES** Wanderer (p. 36) larger with pale spot below apical band on forewing. **STATUS** Common and widespread.

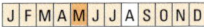

NYMPHALIDAE: HELICONIINAE / BITTER ACRAEAS

## Marsh Acraea
**Moeras-rooitjie**
*Telchinia rahira rahira*   35–50 mm

**HABITS** Low fluttering flight close to food plants. Settles frequently. Fond of flowers. **HABITAT** Marshes in fynbos, karoo, grassland and savanna. **EARLY STAGES** *Egg* barrel-shaped with cross-ribbing. Yellow. Laid in clusters on a leaf of a *Polygonum*, *Persicaria* or *Conyza*. *Larva* up to 33 mm. Dull cream with broad longitudinal grey stripes edged in black. Transverse bands of yellow protuberances carry the black branched spines. Gregarious. *Pupa* up to 17 mm. Cream-white with black-edged yellow spots. Wing veins outlined in black. Attached by the tail to a leaf or twig. **VARIATION** ♂ pale orange. ♀ dark buff. **SIMILAR SPECIES** Orange Acraea (below) deeper orange and ♀ more brightly coloured. **STATUS** Locally common.

J F M A M J J A S O N D

## Orange Acraea
**Oranje-rooitjie**
*Telchinia anacreon*   40–55 mm

**HABITS** Low fluttering flight close to food plants. Fond of flowers. **HABITAT** Riversides and marshes in grassland. **EARLY STAGES** *Egg* a ribbed dome. Yellow, turning brown then purple. Laid in clusters on young shoots of *Cliffortia linearifolia*. *Larva* up to 30 mm. Cylindrical. Two colour morphs, either brown or dull yellow with intermediates. Both morphs have branched black spines. Gregarious. *Pupa* up to 18 mm. Cream-white with black-edged yellow spots. Wing veins outlined in black. Attached by the tail to a leaf or twig. **VARIATION** ♂ orange. ♀ buff with orange markings. **SIMILAR SPECIES** Marsh Acraea (above) is a paler duller orange. Larger Long-winged Orange Acraea (Les., KZN, Mpu. and Lim.) much longer with pointed forewings and doesn't occur near water. **STATUS** Locally common.

J F M A M J J A S O N D

## Dancing Acraea
**Kleinoranje-rooitjie**
*Telchinia serena*  30–44 mm

**HABITS** Weak flight, settling often. May swarm. Fond of flowers. **HABITAT** Savanna and grassland. **EARLY STAGES** *Egg* elongated. Translucent pale yellow, darkening slightly. Laid in clusters on a shoot of one of many food plants, often a *Triumfetta*. *Larva* up to 32 mm. Pale yellow-green to olive green with black-tipped, branched, yellow spines. Gregarious. *Pupa* up to 16 mm. Either white with black-edged yellow spots and wing veins outlined in black, or entirely black with orange spots. Attached by the tail to a leaf or twig. **VARIATION** ♂ orange. ♀ variable combinations of black, orange or brown with white or hyaline forewing patches. **SIMILAR SPECIES** ♂ distinctive. ♀ may resemble several small *Acraea* species, but usually flies with ♂. **STATUS** Common and widespread.

J F M A M J J A S O N D

## Yellow-banded Acraea
**Geelstreep-rooitjie**
*Telchinia cabira*  38–45 mm

**HABITS** Slow, low flight. Fond of flowers. Often gregarious. **HABITAT** Riverine, lowland and escarpment forest. **EARLY STAGES** *Egg* barrel-shaped with cross-ribbing. Translucent yellow. Laid in clusters on the leaf of a *Triumfetta* or *Hermannia*. *Larva* up to 27 mm (♀ larger than ♂). Blue-green with ochre yellow lines and bands. Spines ochre yellow, but black on segments 2, 12 and 13. Gregarious. *Pupa* up to 18 mm. Dirty white with black-edged yellow spots. Wing veins outlined in black. Attached by the tail to a leaf or twig. **VARIATION** Sexes similar. **SIMILAR SPECIES** Dusky Acraea (p. 42) yellowish-cream form told from Yellow-banded Acraea by its distinctive underside. **STATUS** Locally common.

J F M A M J J A S O N D

NYMPHALIDAE: HELICONIINAE / BITTER ACRAEAS 45

## White-barred Acraea
Witstreep-rooitjie
*Telchinia encedon encedon*      **40–55 mm**

**HABITS** Slow low flight. Males gather on hill tops and prominent points. Fond of flowers. **HABITAT** Savanna and forest. **EARLY STAGES** **Egg** barrel-shaped with cross-ribbing. Pale whitish-yellow. Laid in large clusters on the leaves of *Commelina diffusa*. **Larva** up to 33 mm. Dirty grey to black with black spines, a cream to yellow-white lateral band and black dorsal spots. **Pupa** up to 19 mm. Markings not described, but probably similar to those of Dusky Acraea. Attached by the tail to a leaf or twig. **VARIATION** Sexes similar. Several forms: ground colour may be tawny orange, buff or yellow-white, but always has white apical band on upper side forewing. **SIMILAR SPECIES** Tawny orange form resembles a small African Monarch (p. 20), but underside is distinctive. **STATUS** Common and widespread.

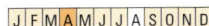

## Polka Dot
Polkastippel
*Pardopsis punctatissima*      **30–36 mm**

**HABITS** Low fluttering flight just above vegetation on grassy hillsides. **HABITAT** Moist grassland, usually close to forest habitat. **EARLY STAGES Egg** domed. Pale yellow. Laid singly on a leaf of *Hybanthus capensis*. **Larva** up to 24 mm. Blue-black to blackish-brown with broken white stripes. Whitish protuberances on all but the fourth segment, where they are black. **Pupa** up to 17 mm. Markings not recorded, but probably similar to an *Acraea*. Suspended head-down from a silk pad. **VARIATION** Sexes similar. **SIMILAR SPECIES** Superficially resembles Spotted Pentila (p. 70). May also be confused with day-flying Leopard Magpie moth (similar distribution), which it seems to mimic. **STATUS** Locally common.

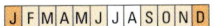

## Blotched Leopard
**Vaalkolluiperd**
*Lachnoptera ayresii* **45–56 mm**

**HABITS** ♂ flies briskly, fairly high up. Patrols forest margins settling often, but restless. ♀ flies lower, near food plants. **HABITAT** Coastal and lower escarpment forest. **EARLY STAGES Egg** a laterally flattened oval with rows of dished depressions. Yellow, developing red bands. Laid singly on a shoot of *Rawsonia lucida*. **Larva** up to 30 mm. Cylindrical with many long, branched black spines. Flesh-pink to yellow with brown to black back stripes and black longitudinal and transverse stripes. **Pupa** up to 20 mm. Bright green or pink. Thorax and abdomen bear several dark-brown spines with red bases. Forms low down on an old leaf. **VARIATION** Sexes similar, but ♀ lacks purple iridescence and ♂ has grey patch of scent scales at apex of hind wing. **SIMILAR SPECIES** Larger than African Leopard (below) with fewer spots. **STATUS** Locally common.

J F M A M J J A S O N D

## African Leopard
**Populierluiperd**
*Phalanta phalantha aethiopica* **40–48 mm**

**HABITS** Fast evasive flight. Pumps wings up and down when settled. **HABITAT** Savanna and woodland. **EARLY STAGES Egg** an elongated oval with vertical rows of depressions. Yellow, turning salmon. Laid singly on a shoot or leaf, often of an exotic *Salix* or *Populus*, but also on a *Dovyalis* or *Oncoba*. **Larva** up to 26 mm. Salmon pink to grey with reddish-brown branched spines. **Pupa** up to 16 mm. Bright green. Black marks may nearly hide the green. Has red-edged silver wing margins as well as warts on thorax and abdomen. **VARIATION** Sexes similar, but ♀ slightly larger, paler and duller. **SIMILAR SPECIES** Forest Leopard (E. Cape, KZN, Mpu., Lim., Swa.) has fewer spots on upper side and more defined marginal markings, and ♀ much duller relative to the ♂ than in African Leopard. **STATUS** Common and widespread.

J F M A M J J A S O N D

## Pearl Charaxes
Pêrel-dubbelstert
*Charaxes varanes varanes*     **65–90 mm**

**HABITS** Patrols forest edges, settling 2–8 m up, lower than other *Charaxes*. Easy to approach. Attracted to rotting fruit. **HABITAT** Savanna, coastal, lowland and escarpment forest. **EARLY STAGES** *Egg* a flat-topped sphere. Pale yellow, turning orange-yellow with an irregular red circlet if fertile. Laid singly on an *Allophylus* or *Searsia* leaf. *Larva* up to 50 mm. Green with horned head shield like other *Charaxes*; has one or two ornate, V-shaped dorsal markings. *Pupa* up to 28 mm. Egg-shaped. Bright blue-green; unmarked except for black spiracles. Hangs by the tail from a silk pad fixed to a leaf. **VARIATION** Sexes similar, but ♀ slightly larger. **SIMILAR SPECIES** The only local *Charaxes* with single tail in both sexes. ♀ Flame-bordered Charaxes (northern KZN) has broad black bands in marginal orange. **STATUS** Common and widespread.

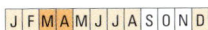

## Green-veined Charaxes
Skelm-dubbelstert
*Charaxes candiope candiope*     **65–95 mm**

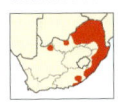

**HABITS** Fast powerful flight in forest canopy. Settles on tree tops. Attracted to fermenting fruit. **HABITAT** Savanna and dry forest. **EARLY STAGES** *Egg* a flat-topped sphere. Pale yellow, darkening and developing red-brown freckles and a darker brown circlet. Laid singly on leaf of a *Croton*. *Larva* up to 50 mm. Bright green with one or two large cream dorsal spots. Horned head shield edged with cream. *Pupa* up to 26 mm. Egg-shaped. Bright green with white blotches on wing cases. Suspended by the tail from a silk pad on a leaf. **VARIATION** Sexes similar, but ♀ larger with two equally long tails. ♂ tails unequal, the anal tails being longer. **SIMILAR SPECIES** None. **STATUS** Common and widespread.

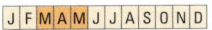

## Flame-bordered Charaxes
Vlam-dubbelstert
*Charaxes protoclea azota*   65–95 mm

**HABITS** Fast powerful flight in forest canopy. Settles on tree tops. Attracted to fermenting fruit. **HABITAT** Coastal sand forest. **EARLY STAGES** *Egg* a flat-topped sphere. Cream, darkening and developing a brown circlet. Laid singly or in pairs on a leaf of *Afzelia quanzensis*. *Larva* up to 60 mm. Bright green, finely speckled with yellow. One or two large, V-shaped, pale yellow-grey dorsal marks. Head shield edged with rusty brown. *Pupa* up to 26 mm. Pale green form has avocado head and thorax. Pale pink form has chocolate head and thorax. Hangs head-down from a silk pad fixed to a leaf. **VARIATION** Sexually dimorphic, as shown. **SIMILAR SPECIES** ♂ unmistakable. In flight ♀ may be mistaken for Pearl Charaxes (p. 47). **STATUS** Rare.

J F M **A M** J J **A S O** N D

## Foxy Charaxes
Koppie-dubbelstert
*Charaxes jasius saturnus*   65–90 mm

**HABITS** Fast gliding flight. Usually seen on hill tops. Attracted to rotting fruit and dung. **HABITAT** Savanna. **EARLY STAGES** *Egg* a flat-topped sphere. Pale yellow, turning green and developing brown circlet. Laid singly on a leaf of *Schotia brachypetala*. *Larva* up to 54 mm. Bright green finely speckled with yellow. One or two large blue dorsal spots with green centres. Pink-tipped head horns. *Pupa* up to 27 mm. Egg-shaped. Bright green with white to pink spots. Hangs head-down from a silk pad fixed to a leaf. **VARIATION** Sexes similar. **SIMILAR SPECIES** Giant Charaxes (p. 49) larger with black ground colour and yellow bands. Protea Charaxes (E., W. and N. Cape) smaller with more underside grey, but favours fynbos and karoo. **STATUS** Common and widespread.

J F **M A M** J **J A S O** N D

## Giant Charaxes
**Reuse-dubbelstert**
*Charaxes castor flavifasciatus*     **75–105 mm**

**HABITS** Fast gliding flight. Usually frequents hill tops before 10h00. Attracted to fermenting fruit and animal dung. **HABITAT** Dry forest and savanna. **EARLY STAGES** *Egg* a flat-topped sphere. Pale yellow, darkening and developing brown circlet. Laid singly on a leaf, often of *Schotia brachypetala* or *Afzelia quanzensis*, but many other plants also suitable. *Larva* up to 90 mm. Bright green, finely speckled with yellow. Has one or two large green dorsal spots with dark centres and pink-tipped head horns. *Pupa* up to 30 mm. Egg-shaped. Bright green with white to pink spots. Hangs head-down from a silk pad fixed to a leaf. **VARIATION** Sexes similar. **SIMILAR SPECIES** Foxy Charaxes (p. 48) smaller with brown ground colour and orange bands. **STATUS** Scarce but widespread.

J F M A M J J A S O N D

## White-barred Charaxes
**Witstreep-dubbelstert**
*Charaxes brutus natalensis*     **60–90 mm**

**HABITS** Fast powerful flight in forest canopy. Settles on tree tops. Attracted to dung and rotting fruit. **HABITAT** Forest and wooded savanna. **EARLY STAGES** *Egg* a flat-topped sphere. Pale cream, darkening and developing pale red-brown freckles and a circlet. Laid singly, usually on a leaf of *Trichilia emetica* or *T. dregeana*, but several other plants also suitable. *Larva* up to 52 mm. Bright green finely speckled with yellow. One or two large yellow dorsal spots. Blue-tipped head horns. *Pupa* up to 26 mm. Cylindrical with squared-off abdomen. Bright green. Hangs head-down from a silk pad fixed to a leaf. **VARIATION** Sexes similar. **SIMILAR SPECIES** Upper side resembles some forms of ♀ Satyr Charaxes (p. 53) or ♀ Scarce Forest Charaxes (p. 52), but undersides very different. **STATUS** Common and widespread.

J F M A M J J A S O N D

## Silver-barred Charaxes
Silwerstreep-dubbelstert
*Charaxes druceanus*                          55–85 mm

**HABITS** Fast powerful flight through forest canopy. Settles on tree tops. Attracted to dung and rotting fruit. **HABITAT** Coastal and escarpment forest. **EARLY STAGES** *Egg* a flat-topped sphere. Pale cream, darkening and developing thin red-brown circlet. Laid singly on a leaf of *Syzygium cordatum*. *Larva* up to 45 mm. Bright green with fine yellow marks and one or two large, semicircular brown dorsal spots. Head shield green edged with yellow. Brown-tipped head horns. *Pupa* up to 30 mm. Egg-shaped. Pale green with red-brown spiracles. Hangs head-down from a silk pad fixed to a leaf. **VARIATION** Sexes similar. Four subspecies in SA, of which the northern ones (not shown) are darker. **SIMILAR SPECIES** Foxy Charaxes (p. 48) has orange bands and lacks silver bars on underside hind wing. **STATUS** Locally common.

## Forest-king Charaxes
Boskoning-dubbelstert
*Charaxes xiphares*                          65–95 mm

**HABITS** Fast, strong, high flight. Settles in tree tops. Fond of sap and rotting fruit. **HABITAT** Afrotemperate forest. **EARLY STAGES** *Egg* a flat-topped sphere. Pale yellow, darkening and developing two thin red-brown circlets. Laid singly on a leaf of *Scutia myrtina* or *Cryptocarya woodii*. *Larva* up to 54 mm. Deep green with fine yellow marks and one or two elliptical brown dorsal spots. Green squared-off head shield and short horns. *Pupa* up to 30 mm. Egg-shaped. Green with fine white streaks. Hangs head-down from a silk pad fixed to a leaf. **VARIATION** Sexually dimorphic, as shown. ♀ upper side hind wing patch is white, mauve or yellow. Nine subspecies in SA, including *occidentalis* and *penningtoni* shown here. **SIMILAR SPECIES** Blue-spotted Charaxes (p. 51) ♂ has white upper side hind wing patch. **STATUS** Locally common.

NYMPHALIDAE: CHARAXINAE / CHARAXES  51

## Blue-spotted Charaxes
Bosprins-dubbelstert
*Charaxes cithaeron cithaeron*    70–95 mm

**HABITS** Fast, strong, high flight. Settles on tree tops. Attracted to tree sap and rotting fruit. **HABITAT** Coastal and lowland riverine forest. **EARLY STAGES** *Egg* a flat-topped sphere. Pale yellow, turning white and developing a circlet of brownish streaks. Laid singly on a *Scutia myrtina* or *Cryptocarya woodii* leaf. *Larva* up to 58 mm. Deep green with fine yellow speckling and one or two circular brown dorsal spots. Green squared-off head shield. Short blue-tipped horns. *Pupa* 28 mm. Egg-shaped. Green with fine cloudy white streaks. Hangs head down from a silk pad fixed to a leaf. **VARIATION** Sexually dimorphic, as shown. **SIMILAR SPECIES** ♀ told from ♀ Forest-king Charaxes (p. 50) ♀ by broad solid, not narrow broken, white band on upper side forewing. ♂ darker with less extensive pale blue than Blue-spotted. **STATUS** Locally common.

J F M A M J J A S O N D

## Club-tailed Charaxes
Wit-en-bruin-dubbelstert
*Charaxes zoolina*    40–58 mm

**HABITS** Flight lower and slower than larger *Charaxes*. Attracted to sap and rotting fruit. **HABITAT** Forest, woodland and savanna. **EARLY STAGES** *Egg* a flat-topped sphere. Pale yellow, darkening and developing purple-brown circlet. Laid singly on a leaf of a climbing *Acacia* like *ataxacantha* or *A. schweinfurthi*. *Larva* up to 45 mm. Bright green with yellow or deep green diagonal stripes. Head shield yellow with green stripes. *Pupa* up to 18 mm. Egg-shaped. Green with fine cloudy white streaks. Hangs head-down from a silk pad fixed to a leaf. **VARIATION** Sexually and seasonally dimorphic, as shown. **SIMILAR SPECIES** On the wing dry season form *neanthes* resembles Blotched Leopard (p. 46). All forms lack pale underside hind wing spots of Pearl-spotted Charaxes (p. 52). **STATUS** Locally common.

J F M A M J J A S O N D

## Pearl-spotted Charaxes
Silwerkol-dubbelstert
*Charaxes jahlusa* 42–62 mm

**HABITS** ♂ avidly defends hill-top territory from a perch in a bush. Both sexes fond of tree sap and rotting fruit. **HABITAT** Savanna, Nama karoo and Albany thicket. **EARLY STAGES** *Egg* oval. Green, darkening and developing a brown circlet. Laid singly, often on *Pappea capensis*. *Larva* up to 35 mm. Green with fine, oblique yellow lateral lines and small yellow-white dorsal spots. Head shield green with short brown-tipped horns. *Pupa* up to 18 mm. Rounded. Pale green with fine cloudy white streaks. Hangs head-down from a silk pad fixed to a leaf. **VARIATION** Sexes similar. Size and extent of underside spots varies among three subspecies. **SIMILAR SPECIES** On the wing like African Leopard (p. 46), which lacks pale spots on underside hind wing. Flies faster than similar-coloured Club-tailed Charaxes form *neanthes* (p. 51). **STATUS** Locally common.

| J | F | M | A | M | J | J | A | S | O | N | D |

## Scarce Forest Charaxes
Seldsame bos-dubbelstert
*Charaxes etesipe tavetensis* 55–72 mm

**HABITS** Attracted to tree sap and fermenting fruit. ♂ patrols river beds for animal and bird droppings. **HABITAT** Sand and lowland riverine forest. **EARLY STAGES** *Egg* a flat-topped sphere. White, turning yellow and developing a brown circlet. Laid singly on a leaf of *Afzelia quanzensis* or *Margaritaria discoidea*. *Larva* up to 60 mm. Dull blue-green with white speckling. Diamond- or crescent-shaped yellow-white dorsal spots. Green head shield and black-tipped horns. *Pupa* up to 24 mm. Egg-shaped. Deep green with cream-white stripes. Hangs head-down from a silk pad fixed to a leaf. **VARIATION** Sexually dimorphic, as shown. **SIMILAR SPECIES** Underside like Bushveld Charaxes (p. 53), but hind wing bulges out at anal angle. ♀ upper side resembles that of White-barred Charaxes (p. 49). **STATUS** Rare.

| J | F | M | A | M | J | J | A | S | O | N | D |

## Bushveld Charaxes
**Bosveld-dubbelstert**
*Charaxes achaemenes achaemenes*   **55–70 mm**

**HABITS** Strong flight. Attracted to tree sap and fermenting fruit. ♂ aggressively defends hill-top territory. **HABITAT** Savanna. **EARLY STAGES** *Egg* a flat-topped sphere. Yellow-white, turning green and developing a brown circlet. Laid singly on a leaf of a *Pterocarpus* or a *Dalbergia*. *Larva* up to 50 mm. Green with variable number of brown-edged white dorsal spots in transverse rows. Head shield green with brown-tipped horns. *Pupa* up to 21 mm. Egg-shaped. Bright green with prominent yellow stripes. Hangs head-down from a silk pad fixed to a leaf. **VARIATION** Sexually dimorphic, as shown. **SIMILAR SPECIES** Underside like that of Scarce Forest Charaxes (p. 52), but outer margin of hind wing more evenly curved. In ♂, upper side resembles that of White-barred Charaxes (p. 49). **STATUS** Common and widespread.

J F M A M J J A S O N D

## Satyr Charaxes
**Kus-dubbelstert**
*Charaxes ethalion ethalion*   **45–63 mm**

**HABITS** Rapid flight, settling in tree tops. Fond of sap and rotting fruit. **HABITAT** Lowland and coastal forest and savanna. **EARLY STAGES** *Egg* a flat-topped sphere. Pale yellow, darkening and developing a brown circlet. Laid singly on *Albizia adianthifolia*. *Larva* up to 40 mm. Green with variable, U-shaped, blue-edged white dorsal marks. Head shield green. Horns brown-tipped. *Pupa* up to 23 mm. Egg-shaped. Pale green with fine yellow wing line. Hangs head-down from a silk pad fixed to a leaf. **VARIATION** Sexually dimorphic, as shown. ♀ polymorphic. **SIMILAR SPECIES** Pondo (E. Cape, southern KZN), Marieps (Mpu., southern Lim.) and Karkloof (KZN to W. Cape) charaxes. Van Son's (northern KZN, Lim. and NW) and Demon (northern KZN to Lim.) charaxes only in dry savanna. **STATUS** Common and widespread.

J F M A M J J A S O N D

## Forest Queen
**Boskoningin**
*Charaxes wakefieldi*                 **65–90 mm**

**HABITS** Slow gliding flight in semi-shade. Fond of fermenting fruit. **HABITAT** Lowland and coastal forest. **EARLY STAGES** *Egg* a flat-topped sphere. Pale yellow, turning brown if fertile. Laid singly on a leaf of *Deinbollia oblongifolia*. *Larva* up to 50 mm. Fat with sharply tapered tail. Green with white edges and two raised, elliptical, cream-white dorsal marks. Head shield green with cream to brown horns; outer pair wider set than in other *Charaxes*. *Pupa* 24 mm. Angular. Shiny green with fine white streaks. Hangs by tail from a leaf or twig. **VARIATION** Sexually dimorphic, as shown. **SIMILAR SPECIES** ♂ mimics Blue (Dappled) Monarch (rare vagrant) and resembles Veined Swordtail (p. 130). ♀ mimics Friar (p. 20). Both sexes told from these similar species by yellow abdomen. **STATUS** Scarce and local.

## Battling Glider
**Alsie-witkoppie**
*Cymothoe alcimeda*               **40–55 mm**

**HABITS** ♂ flight gliding with jerky wing beats. Perches high up on forest margin. ♀ flutters in semi-shade. Attracted to damp sand. **HABITAT** Escarpment forest. **EARLY STAGES** *Egg* domed with hexagonal indents. Transparent white. Laid in clusters on *Kiggelaria africana*. *Larva* up to 35 mm. Green or dull yellow with branched, black-tipped, yellow spines. Gregarious at first, but solitary later. *Pupa* up to 14 mm. Angular with keeled thorax and abdomen. Shiny green with yellow line along wing cases. Hangs by tail from a leaf or twig. **VARIATION** Sexually dimorphic, as shown. Five subspecies. ♀ polymorphic, with white, yellow or orange bands. **SIMILAR SPECIES** Larger Blonde Glider (p. 55) occurs in lower altitude forests. Orange-banded ♀ form superficially like Southern Short-tailed Admiral (p. 68). **STATUS** Locally common.

NYMPHALIDAE: LIMENITINAE / GLIDERS, NYMPHS

## Blonde Glider
Cora-witkoppie
*Cymothoe coranus*        **50–68 mm**

**HABITS** ♂ glides with sudden jerky wing beats. Patrols forest edge, perching high up. ♀ flutters in semi-shade. Both sexes attracted to damp sand and fermenting fruit. **HABITAT** Coastal, lowland forest and low-altitude Afrotemperate forest. **EARLY STAGES** *Egg* domed with hexagonal indentations. Transparent white. Laid in clusters on a leaf of *Rawsonia lucida*. *Larva* up to 45 mm. Brownish-green with branched black spines. Gregarious in early stages, but solitary when full-grown. *Pupa* up to 18 mm. Resembles Battling Glider pupa, but larger with red along dorsal keel. **VARIATION** Sexually dimorphic, as shown. **SIMILAR SPECIES** Could be confused with smaller Battling Glider (p. 54) in the few areas where their Afrotemperate forest ranges overlap. **STATUS** Locally common.

## Mottled-green Nymph
Bosdansertjie
*Euryphura achlys*        **48–65 mm**

**HABITS** Low gliding flight. Fast if disturbed. Favours forest paths and glades near streams. Feeds on rotting fruit. **HABITAT** Coastal and lowland forest. **EARLY STAGES** *Egg* domed and multifaceted. Gold-green. Laid singly on a leaf of *Erythroxyon emarginatum*. *Larva* up to 35 mm. Bluish-green with long feathery lateral spines that make it hard to spot. A row of diamond-shaped, pink-centred white spots runs along the back. *Pupa* up to 24 mm. Shiny green with keeled wing cases, each with a metallic gold spot. **VARIATION** Slight sexual dimorphism; note female's white wing-tip band. **SIMILAR SPECIES** Guinea-fowl Butterfly (p. 56) has similar habits and markings, but upper side is grey, not green. **STATUS** Rare.

**NYMPHALIDAE: LIMENITINAE / FORESTERS**

## Gold-banded Forester
Skaduweedansertjie
*Euphaedra neophron neophron*   55–78 mm

**HABITS** Low gliding flight, but fast when disturbed. Wary and difficult to approach closely. Frequents forest pathways and glades, feeding on fermenting fruit. **HABITAT** Coastal and lowland forest. **EARLY STAGES** *Egg* a flattened sphere. Cream-yellow, turning black as larva develops. Laid singly on a leaf of *Deinbollia oblongifolia*. *Larva* up to 55 mm. Sage green with long feathery lateral spines that provide good camouflage. A row of dark spots runs down the back. *Pupa* up to 30 mm. Angular. Shiny translucent green with metallic gold spots. Hangs by tail from a leaf or twig. **VARIATION** Sexes similar. **SIMILAR SPECIES** None. **STATUS** Locally common.

| J | F | M | A | M | J | J | A | S | O | N | D |

## Guinea-fowl Butterfly
Tarentaaltjie
*Hamanumida daedalus*   55–78 mm

**HABITS** Low, gliding flight, but rapid if disturbed. Wary and difficult to approach. Frequents paths and bare ground, settling open winged. Attracted to rotting fruit. **HABITAT** Savanna. **EARLY STAGES** *Egg* a multifaceted flattened sphere. Translucent green-white; develops red band as larva grows. Laid singly on leaf of a *Combretum* or *Terminalia*. *Larva* up to 30 mm. Leaf green with long, feathery lateral spines that provide camouflage. Pink stripe runs down the back. *Pupa* up to 24 mm. A pointed oval. Shiny and translucent with both a green and a lilac form. Hangs by tail from a leaf or twig. **VARIATION** Sexes similar. Wet season form *meleagris* (not shown) has white underside spots. **SIMILAR SPECIES** Mottled-green Nymph (p. 55) is green, not grey, and is confined to Maputaland. **STATUS** Common and widespread.

| J | F | M | A | M | J | J | A | S | O | N | D |

## Trimen's False Acraea
**Trimen-se-valsrooitjie**
*Pseudacraea boisduvalii trimenii* **65–88 mm**

**HABITS** Sailing flight across forest clearings. Settles high up and chases away intruders. ♂ also seen on hill tops. Attracted to fermenting fruit. **HABITAT** Coastal, riverine and escarpment forest. **EARLY STAGES** *Egg* a multifaceted dome. Translucent green-white, turning golden yellow. Laid singly on a leaf of *Englerophytum* or *Mimusops*. *Larva* up to 45 mm. Well camouflaged to resemble lichen-covered twig. Black-brown with horned processes on thorax and tail and patches of greenish-white and brown. *Pupa* up to 37 mm. Elongated and pointed at both ends. Green. Hangs by tail from a leaf or twig. **VARIATION** Sexes similar. Form *colvillei* has translucent apical patches on forewing. **SIMILAR SPECIES** Mimics Acara Acraea (p. 40), but is much larger and more robustly built. **STATUS** Locally common.

*colvillei*

*trimenii*

*trimenii*

J F M A M J J A S O N D

## False Wanderer
**Skaduwee-valsrooitjie**
*Pseudacraea eurytus imitator* **60–75 mm**

**HABITS** Sailing flight across forest clearings. Settles high up and chases intruders. Often seen under canopy. **HABITAT** Coastal and escarpment forest. **EARLY STAGES** *Egg* a multifaceted dome. Salmon pink, turning brown. Laid singly on leaf of an *Englerophytum* or *Mimusops*. *Larva* up to 40 mm. Camouflaged to resemble forest debris. Mottled olive-green with patches of greenish-white and brown. Green horned processes on thorax and tail. *Pupa* up to 32 mm. Elongated and pointed at both ends. Green. Hangs by tail from a leaf or twig. **VARIATION** Sexually dimorphic, as shown. Rare ♂ form *pondo* (not shown) is orange, not cream. **SIMILAR SPECIES** Effectively mimics Wanderer (p. 36) but has dark-ringed basal spots on upper side hind and forewings. **STATUS** Scarce and local.

J F M A M J J A S O N D

*tarquinia*

*tarquinia*

## False Chief
Bont-valsrooitjie
*Pseudacraea lucretia*  60–78 mm

**HABITS** Sailing flight. Often seen under forest canopy. Settles high up and chases intruders. **HABITAT** Coastal and escarpment forest. **EARLY STAGES** *Egg* domed and multifaceted. Yellow, developing brown ring. Laid singly on a leaf of an *Englerophytum* or *Mimusops*. *Larva* up to 40 mm. Green above, white below with red lateral stripe and two large red-brown horns protruding at 45° from thorax. Short branched green spines along body. *Pupa* up to 32 mm. Elongated, pointed at both ends, with dorsal fin. Green. Hangs by tail from a leaf or twig. **VARIATION** Sexes similar. Pale markings range from white to buff or orange and are more extensive in northern race *expansa* than in southern race *tarquinia*. **SIMILAR SPECIES** Mimics Chief (p. 22), but has rougher edges to pale spots. **STATUS** Locally common.

J F M A M J J A S O N D

## Spotted Sailer
Spikkel-swerwer
*Neptis saclava marpessa*  40–48 mm

**HABITS** Slow sailing flight through woodland glades and clearings. Holds wings flat, flapping occasionally. **HABITAT** Woodland, forest and watercourses in arid areas. **EARLY STAGES** *Egg* domed and multifaceted. Pale green. Laid singly on *Acalypha glabrata*, *Combretum bracteosum* or *Ricinus communis*. *Larva* up to 21 mm. Camouflaged to resemble leaf debris. Mottled drab green with horny processes on thorax. Rests doubled over. *Pupa* up to 13 mm. Wing cases sharply keeled. Resembles a dead leaf. Fawn with shiny golden patches. Hangs by tail from a leaf or twig. **VARIATION** Sexes similar. **SIMILAR SPECIES** Smaller than Common Sailer (p. 59). Pale-edged spots along upper side hind wing margin are unique among SA's six sailers. **STATUS** Common and widespread.

J F M A M J J A S O N D

## Common Sailer
Reënbos-swerwer
*Neptis laeta*            **40–52 mm**

**HABITS** Slow sailing flight in clearings. Holds wings flat and gives few wing beats. **HABITAT** Forest and wooded savanna along coast and escarpment. **EARLY STAGES** *Egg* a multifaceted dome. Pale yellow-green. Laid singly on *Dalbergia obovata*, *D. armata*, *Albizia adianthifolia* or an *Acalypha*. *Larva* up to 27 mm. Resembles leaf debris. Mottled green with horny processes on thorax. Rests doubled over. *Pupa* up to 15 mm. Wing cases sharply keeled. Also resembles dead leaf. Fawn with shiny gold patches. Hangs by tail from a leaf or twig. **VARIATION** Sexes similar. **SIMILAR SPECIES** Larger and darker than Spotted Sailer (p. 58). Very similar to Barred (E. Cape, Pondoland) and Kiriakoff's (northern Lim.) sailers. Larger than Streaked (KZN, Mpu., Lim.) and Jordan's (northern KZN) sailers. **STATUS** Common and widespread.

J F M A M J J A S O N D

## Boisduval's Tree Nymph
Boisduval-se-boombruintjie
*Sevenia boisduvali boisduvali*      **35–45 mm**

**HABITS** Glides with few wing beats in clearings. Settles with open wings. Fond of tree sap and rotting fruit. May swarm in thousands. **HABITAT** Forest and wooded savanna on coast and escarpment. **EARLY STAGES** *Egg* domed. Yellow. Laid in large clusters on *Sclerocroton integerrimum* or *Shirakiopsis elliptica*. *Larva* up to 22 mm. Cylindrical. Tawny orange with black longitudinal stripes and branched spines. Gregarious. *Pupa* up to 13 mm. Elongated with squared thorax. Plain green to variegated brown-black. Hangs by tail from a leaf or twig. **VARIATION** Sexually dimorphic, as shown. **SIMILAR SPECIES** Natal Tree Nymph (p. 60) larger and more brightly coloured. Morant's Tree Nymph (eastern KZN, Mpu., northern Lim., Swa.) larger, paler, with flatter underside. **STATUS** Common and widespread.

J F M A M J J A S O N D

## Natal Tree Nymph
**Natal-boombruintjie**
*Sevenia natalensis*     40–48 mm

**HABITS** Glides with few wing beats through forest glades and clearings. Often settles open-winged on bark. Fond of tree sap and rotting fruit. May swarm in thousands. **HABITAT** Forest and wooded savanna. **EARLY STAGES** *Egg* domed. Yellow. Laid singly on *Sclerocroton integerrimus* or *Shirakiopsis elliptica*. *Larva* up to 27 mm. Tawny orange with black longitudinal stripes and branched spines. *Pupa* 15 mm. Elongated with squared thorax. Bright green with yellow line along wing cases. **VARIATION** Sexually dimorphic, as shown. **SIMILAR SPECIES** Boisduval's Tree Nymph (p. 59) smaller and darker. Morant's Tree Nymph (eastern KZN, Mpu., northern Lim., Swa.) dull brown with fainter underside markings. **STATUS** Common and widespread.

J F **M A M J J A S** O N D

## Spotted Joker
**Leliegrasvegter**
*Byblia ilithyia*     38–45 mm

**HABITS** Glides low with few wing beats. ♂ territorial. Fond of rotting fruit. May suck grass flowers. **HABITAT** Grassland and dry savanna. **EARLY STAGES** *Egg* onion-shaped, with erect hairs. Cream-yellow. Laid singly on *Tragia glabrata* or *Dalechampia capensis*. *Larva* up to 32 mm. Tapers. Large double head horns. Tawny orange with broad black longitudinal stripes and branched spines. *Pupa* up to 18 mm. Elongated with squared thorax. Brown or green with countershading. Hangs by tail from a leaf or twig. **VARIATION** Sexes similar but in ♀ orange is suffused with dark brown. Nominate wet season form told from dry season form *badiata* by pure orange underside bands and broader white stripes. **SIMILAR SPECIES** Less widespread Joker (similar distribution) lacks discal spots on upper side hind wing. **STATUS** Common and widespread.

J **F M A M** J J **A S O N** D

**NYMPHALIDAE**: BIBLIDINAE / PIPERS

## Pied Piper
**Witlint-bosvlieër**
*Eurytela hiarbas angustata*     **45–55 mm**

**HABITS** Wary, gliding flight at forest margins. Seems to flip on and off perches. Settles often with open wings. **HABITAT** Disturbed areas of forest. **EARLY STAGES** *Egg* onion-shaped and covered in erect hairs. Pale green. Laid singly on a *Tragia*, *Dalechampia capensis* or *Ricinus communis*. *Larva* up to 30 mm. Cylindrical with large double head horns. Various shades of drab green, grey or brown with paler sides and branched spines. *Pupa* up to 18 mm. Elongated with keeled wing cases. Brown to green. Hangs from a silk pad fixed to a leaf or twig. **VARIATION** Sexes similar. **SIMILAR SPECIES** Superficially resembles a sailer on the wing. **STATUS** Common and widespread.

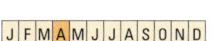

## Golden Piper
**Oranjelint-bosvlieër**
*Eurytela dryope angulata*     **40–55 mm**

**HABITS** Wary, gliding flight around forest edges. Seems to flip on and off perches. Settles often with wings open. **HABITAT** Disturbed areas in forests. **EARLY STAGES** *Egg* onion-shaped and covered in erect hairs. Pale green. Laid singly on a *Tragia*, *Dalechampia capensis* or *Ricinus communis*. *Larva* up to 30 mm. Bears large double horns. Various shades of drab green, grey or brown with paler sides and branched spines. *Pupa* up to 18 mm. Elongated with keeled wing cases. Brown to green. Hangs from a silk pad fixed to leaf or twig. **VARIATION** Sexes similar. **SIMILAR SPECIES** Dead-leaf (Eared) Commodore (p. 65) is larger with dark spots within orange bands. Soldier Pansy's (p. 66) forewing is not hooked. **STATUS** Locally common.

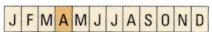

## Common Diadem
**Blouglans (♂) Na-aper (♀)**
*Hypolimnas misippus*  60–80 mm

**HABITS** ♂ flight rapid and evasive, often on hill tops. ♀ more leisurely. Both attracted to flowers. **HABITAT** Savanna, grassland and urban areas. Also, rarely, in succulent karoo. **EARLY STAGES** *Egg* domed and ribbed. Green. Laid singly on a shoot of *Asystasia gangetica*, another of the Acanthaceae or one of many other plants, often a *Portulaca*. *Larva* up to 50 mm. Black and spiny with orange side stripes and head. *Pupa* up to 25 mm. Mottled brown with brown to gold dorsal spines. Hangs head-down from a leaf or twig. **VARIATION** Sexually dimorphic, as shown. ♀ polymorphic: forms with white upper side hind wing patches or orange upper side forewing tips are common. **SIMILAR SPECIES** ♂ unique. ♀ a good mimic of African Monarch (p. 20), but has scalloped wing edges and is more alert. **STATUS** Common and widespread.

J F M A M J J A S O N D

## Variable Diadem
**Verneukertjie**
*Hypolimnas anthedon wahlbergi*  75–90 mm

**HABITS** Normal flight is slow and leisurely like that of the distasteful Friar and Layman (species that it mimics). Flies fast if molested. **HABITAT** Forest and heavily wooded savanna. **EARLY STAGES** *Egg* domed and ribbed. Dull yellow-green. Laid in clusters of 2–4 on a shoot of *Laportea peduncularis*. *Larva* up to 50 mm. Cylindrical. Black with long orange branched spines and head horns. *Pupa* up to 27 mm. Mottled black-brown with dorsal spines. Hangs head-down from a leaf or twig. **VARIATION** Sexes similar. Form *mima* mimics Layman. Nominate *wahlbergi* mimics Friar. **SIMILAR SPECIES** Mimics Friar (p. 20) and Layman (p. 21). The rare Deceptive Diadem (KZN to E. Cape coast) resembles form *mima*, but has more angular white marks. **STATUS** Locally common.

J F M A M J J A S O N D

## Mother-of-pearl
Perlemoenskoenlapper
*Protogoniomorpha parhassus*     **65–90 mm**

**HABITS** Flapping, swooping flight. May congregate in riverine bush. ♂ territorial. ♀ seen near food plants. **HABITAT** Lowland and riverine forest. **EARLY STAGES** *Egg* domed and ribbed. Pale green. Laid singly on a young shoot of *Phaulopsis imbricata*, *Asystasia gangetica*, or another of the Acanthaceae. *Larva* up to 56 mm. Cylindrical. Brown with salmon pink transverse bands and branched brown spines. *Pupa* up to 30 mm. Brown with gold spots and dorsal spines. Hangs head-down from a leaf or twig. **VARIATION** Sexes similar. Dry season form (not shown) is smaller and darker. **SIMILAR SPECIES** Clouded Mother-of-Pearl (E. Cape to Lim.) is rarer, smaller, with more extensive dark wing areas and the ♀ has a cream and a white form. **STATUS** Common and widespread.

♂

♂

## Pirate
Seerower
*Catacroptera cloanthe cloanthe*     **50–62 cm**

**HABITS** Flight low, gliding, but fast. Seems to flip on and off perches. Usually occurs singly in open grassland. Settles often on rocks or bare ground. **HABITAT** Grassland and savanna. Favours damp areas. **EARLY STAGES** *Egg* domed and ribbed. Pale green. Laid singly on a young shoot of a *Ruellia*, *Chaetacanthus setiger*, or another of the grassland Acanthaceae. *Larva* up to 45 mm. Twin clubbed head processes. Yellow-brown with black transverse bands and branched spines. *Pupa* up to 26 mm. Green with black dots and dorsal spines. Hangs head-down from a leaf or twig. **VARIATION** Sexes similar. Nominate, wet season, form has orange-buff underside. Dry season form *obscurior* is darker with chocolate brown underside. **SIMILAR SPECIES** Tawnier than Gaudy Commodore form *natalensis* (p. 64). **STATUS** Locally common.

♂ / obscurior

♀

## Gaudy Commodore
**Rooi-en-blou-blaarvlerk**
*Precis octavia sesamus*         **50–63 mm**

**HABITS** Fast gliding flight. Flips on and off perches. Dry season form *sesamus* hibernates in the shade of walls and stream banks. Wet season form *natalensis* congregates on hill tops. **HABITAT** Grassland and savanna, especially rocky slopes. **EARLY STAGES** *Egg* a ribbed dome. Pale green. Laid singly on a shoot of a *Plectranthus*, *Pycnostachys* or another of the grassland Lamiaceae. *Larva* up to 45 mm. Cylindrical with branched spines and twin head processes. Dark brown to black with tawny transverse bands varying in width. *Pupa* up to 26 mm. Carries dorsal spines. Brown burnished with gold. Hangs head-down from a leaf or twig. **VARIATION** Sexes similar. Seasonally dimorphic, as shown. **SIMILAR SPECIES** Distinctive. Form *natalensis* may be mistaken for Pirate (p. 63). **STATUS** Common and widespread.

## Garden Commodore
**Rotsblaarvlerk**
*Precis archesia*         **45–60 mm**

**HABITS** Fast, gliding flight. Seems to flip on and off perches. Both seasonal forms occur on hill tops, in open country and in gardens. **HABITAT** Grassland and savanna, especially rocky slopes. **EARLY STAGES** *Egg* a ribbed dome. Yellow-green. Laid singly on a young shoot of a *Plectranthus*. *Larva* up to 45 mm. Dark grey-brown to black with branched, black-tipped, yellow-orange spines and twin black head processes. *Pupa* up to 26 mm. Black with silver dorsal spines. Hangs head-down from a leaf or twig. **VARIATION** Sexes similar. Seasonally dimorphic, as shown. **SIMILAR SPECIES** Wet season form *pelasgis* may be mistaken for one of the orange-banded Nymphalids, but is distinguished by wing shape. **STATUS** Common and widespread.

## Dead-leaf (Eared) Commodore
**Tugela-blaarvlerk**
*Precis tugela tugela*   **55–64 mm**

**HABITS** Low gliding flight. Flaps infrequently. Settles often with open wings. Heads for canopy when disturbed. ♂ territorial. Nominate dry season form *tugela* congregates in holes in embankments. **HABITAT** Forest and woodland. **EARLY STAGES** *Egg* a ribbed dome. Pale green. Laid singly on a young shoot of a *Plectranthus* or *Pycnostachys*. *Larva* up to 45 mm. Brown marked with variable amounts of black. Branched, black-tipped, cream-white spines and twin black head processes. *Pupa* up to 26 mm. Brown-black, burnished with silver-gold. Gold dorsal spines. Hangs head-down from a leaf or twig. **VARIATION** Sexes similar. Dry season form *aurorina* (not shown) has shorter 'ears' on forewing tips. **SIMILAR SPECIES** Soldier Pansy (p. 66) is smaller with no black spots in the orange bands. **STATUS** Locally common.

## Brown Commodore
**Natal-gesiggie**
*Junonia natalica natalica*   **45–55 mm**

**HABITS** Low fluttering flight in open areas. Settles often, slowly opening and closing wings. **HABITAT** Forest and wooded savanna in lowland areas. **EARLY STAGES** *Egg* a ribbed dome. Green. Laid singly on a growth shoot of a food plant like *Dyschoriste depressa*, *Ruellia patula*, *Justicia* or another low-growing herb in the Acanthaceae. *Larva* up to 38 mm. Cylindrical. Black and spiny with orange head. *Pupa* up to 20 mm. Yellow to grey-brown. Hangs head-down from a leaf or twig. **VARIATION** Sexes similar, but ♂ has less orange on upper side. Nominate dry season form has darker plainer underside than wet season form (not shown). **SIMILAR SPECIES** None. **STATUS** Locally common.

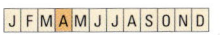

## Soldier Pansy
**Bosgesiggie**
*Junonia terea elgiva* 50–60 mm

**HABITS** Low flight along shady pathways and clearings. Settles often, slowly opening and closing wings. **HABITAT** The understorey of lowland coastal forest as well as wooded areas along rivers. **EARLY STAGES** *Egg* a ribbed dome. Green. Laid singly on a growth shoot of a food plant like *Dyschoriste depressa*, *Ruellia patula* or another low-growing herb in the Acanthaceae. *Larva* up to 35 mm. Black and spiny with orange head. *Pupa* up to 20 mm. Brown with pale markings. Hangs head-down from a leaf or twig. **VARIATION** Sexes similar. Dry season form (not shown) has darker, plainer underside. **SIMILAR SPECIES** Dead-leaf (Eared) Commodore (p. 65) is larger with black spots in orange bands, which are paler than those of Soldier Pansy. **STATUS** Locally common.

J F M A M J J A S O N D

## Yellow Pansy
**Geel-gesiggie**
*Junonia hierta cebrene* 40–50 mm

**HABITS** Low fast flight. Frequently returns to the same spot. A sun-loving, active, but confiding garden butterfly. **HABITAT** Open country, woodland, savanna, grassland and karoo vegetation. **EARLY STAGES** *Egg* a ribbed dome. Green. Laid singly on a growth shoot of a food plant like *Barleria obtusa*, *Dyschoriste depressa*, *Ruellia cordata* or another low-growing herb in the Acanthaceae. *Larva* up to 42 mm. Cylindrical. Grey-brown with black spines. *Pupa* up to 20 mm. Brown to grey with pale markings. Hangs head-down from a leaf or twig. **VARIATION** Sexes similar, but ♂ lacks black bars on upper side forewing, has brighter yellow patches and lacks eyespots in patch on upper side hind wing. **SIMILAR SPECIES** None. **STATUS** Common and widespread.

J F M A M J J A S O N D

**NYMPHALIDAE**: NYMPHALINAE / PANSIES

## Blue Pansy
**Blou-gesiggie**
*Junonia oenone oenone*      **40–52 cm**

**HABITS** Very fast flight. ♂ highly aggressive in defending elevated territory. May chase away large butterflies like *Charaxes*. **HABITAT** Forest, woodland, savanna and, sometimes, grassland and karoo vegetation. **EARLY STAGES** *Egg* a ribbed dome. Green. Laid singly on a shoot of a food plant such as *Asystasia gangetica* or *Dyschoriste depressa*, or on a *Justicia*, *Barleria* or other low-growing herb in the Acanthaceae. *Larva* up to 42 mm. Grey-brown with black spines. *Pupa* up to 20 mm. Brown to grey with pale markings. Hangs head-down from a leaf or twig. **VARIATION** Sexes similar, but ♀ has more and better defined red eyespots. **SIMILAR SPECIES** Eyed Pansy (below) has far more blue on upper side. **STATUS** Common and widespread.

## Eyed Pansy
**Padwagtertjie**
*Junonia orithya madagascariensis*      **38–48 mm**

**HABITS** Low fast flight. Returns frequently to the same spot. Usually found singly, but may swarm in large numbers. **HABITAT** Grassland and grassy areas near forest habitat. **EARLY STAGES** *Egg* a pale, transparent green, ribbed dome. Laid singly on a young shoot of one of many Acanthaceae or Scrophulariaceae. *Graderia subintegra* seems to be main food plant. *Larva* up to 37 mm. Cylindrical. Blue-grey with orange lateral band and black spines. *Pupa* up to 20 mm. Ochreous-brown with darker markings. Hangs head-down from a leaf or twig. **VARIATION** Sexes similar, but ♀ has more red eyespots. **SIMILAR SPECIES** In Blue Pansy (above) blue is restricted to spot on upper side hind wing. **STATUS** Locally common.

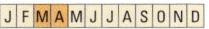

## Painted Lady
Sondagsrokkie
*Vanessa cardui*            40–50 mm

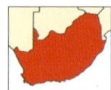

**HABITS** Glides close to the ground, flapping infrequently. May swarm on flowers in large numbers. ♂ competes for hill-top territory. **HABITAT** Occurs in all biomes, throughout SA, but less common in deserts and dense forest. **EARLY STAGES** *Egg* a ribbed dome. Laid singly on a wide range of plants, predominantly Asteraceae. Main food plants are gazanias, *Cirsium vulgare* and *Berkheya bipinnatifida*. *Larva* up to 30 mm. Cylindrical. Black-brown to pink, green, grey or buff. Covered in branched spines that may be white, pink, dirty buff or black. *Pupa* up to 22 mm. Varies from pale brown to shades of grey or pinkish-buff, burnished with gold. Hangs head-down from a leaf or twig. **VARIATION** Sexes similar. **SIMILAR SPECIES** None. **STATUS** Common and widespread.

| J | F | M | A | M | J | J | A | S | O | N | D |

## Southern Short-tailed Admiral
Suidelike-bosnooientjie
*Vanessa hippomene hippomene*     40–48 mm

**HABITS** Rapid gliding flight. Flaps infrequently. Patrols forest canopy and margins. Settles often with wings at 45°. Wary. **HABITAT** Coastal and escarpment forest and wooded valleys near the coast. **EARLY STAGES** *Egg* a ribbed dome. Transparent green. Laid singly on *Laportea peduncularis*. *Larva* up to 30 mm. Cylindrical. Black-brown with branched black spines. *Pupa* up to 22 mm. Elongated with short dorsal spines on abdomen and thorax. Ochreous-brown with darker markings. Hangs head-down from a leaf or twig. **VARIATION** Sexes similar. **SIMILAR SPECIES** Long-tailed Admiral (E. Cape to Lim.) is larger with longer tails and reddish underside hind wing. Northern Short-tailed Admiral (Swa. to Lim.) is similar but upper side bands are red-orange and upper side forewing band does not narrow to a point at inner margin. **STATUS** Scarce but widespread.

| J | F | M | A | M | J | J | A | S | O | N | D |

**NYMPHALIDAE:** LIBYTHEINAE / SNOUTS, ZULUS

# African Snout
**Snuitskoenlapper**
*Libythea labdaca laius*          **40–50 mm**

**HABITS** Fast erratic flight when disturbed. Otherwise rests head-down, wings closed, on dead twigs, bark or the ground. Antennae point forward along the 'snout' (actually its palpi) so that it resembles a dead leaf. **HABITAT** Coastal and escarpment forest. **EARLY STAGES** *Egg* ribbed and bottle-shaped. White, turning brown as larva develops. Laid singly on a leaf of white stinkwood *Celtis africana*. *Larva* up to 22 mm. Brown with cream and white longitudinal stripes. Rests with front segments raised. *Pupa* up to 13 mm. Stubby. Green with a point on the thorax where the wing cases meet dorsally. Forms among leaves or on bark. **VARIATION** Sexes similar. **SIMILAR SPECIES** None. **STATUS** Scarce but widespread.

J F M A M J J A S O N D

# Yellow Zulu
**Geel-zoeloe**
*Alaena amazoula*          **22–32 mm**

**HABITS** Colonial. Low, weak, fluttering flight among grass on rocky slopes. Settles often. **HABITAT** Savanna, grassland and grassy areas adjacent to forest. **EARLY STAGES** *Egg* bun-shaped with concentric rings of pits. Black. Laid singly or in short rows on dead twigs or grass stems near edible lichen. *Larva* up to 16 mm. Slug-shaped and covered in hairs. Cream with grey and buff patterns. *Pupa* up to 13 mm. Stubby and also hairy. Grey-white with brown-black transverse bands. Forms on dry vegetation or rocks. **VARIATION** ♀ has less black on upper side. Northern subspecies *ochroma* (not shown) has more dark scaling on wing veins than nominate. **SIMILAR SPECIES** None. **STATUS** Scarce but widespread.

J F M A M J J A S O N D

### Spotted Pentila
Spikkel-geelvlerkie
*Pentila tropicalis*  29–44 mm

**HABITS** Weak fluttering flight in shade of forest canopy. Small groups often perch together. **HABITAT** Coastal and lowland forest. **EARLY STAGES** *Egg* bun-shaped with concentric rings of pits. Brown. Laid singly on tree bark or leaves near edible lichen. *Larva* details not fully recorded, but slug-shaped and covered in long brown hairs. *Pupa* details not recorded. **VARIATION** Sexes similar. Northern subspecies *fuscipunctata* (not shown) has more extensive dark markings than nominate. **SIMILAR SPECIES** Zulu Buff (KZN, Maputaland) has sparser, better defined black spots. Natal (below) and Pennington's (p. 71) buffs have darker underside hind wings. **STATUS** Scarce but widespread.

| J | F | M | A | M | J | J | A | S | O | N | D |

### Natal Buff
Natalse-boomgeelvlerkie
*Baliochila aslanga*  23–31 cm

**HABITS** Weak fluttering flight in shade of forest canopy. Small groups perch together, slowly opening and closing their wings while sucking honeydew from scale insects. **HABITAT** Coastal and lowland forest. **EARLY STAGES** *Egg* bun-shaped with pits arranged in concentric rings. Pinkish-buff. Laid singly on bark or leaves near edible lichen. *Larva* details not fully recorded, but slug-shaped, pale grey and covered in long hairs. *Pupa* details not recorded. **VARIATION** Sexually dimorphic, as shown. **SIMILAR SPECIES** Pennington's Buff (p. 71) has flatter underside. Both sexes of Lipara Buff (northern KZN, Maputaland) resemble ♀ Natal Buff, but are smaller and darker. **STATUS** Scarce and local.

| J | F | M | A | M | J | J | A | S | O | N | D |

LYCAENIDAE: PORITIINAE / BUFFS, ROCKSITTERS

## Pennington's Buff
Pennington-se-boomgeelvlerkie
*Cnodontes penningtoni*     **23–29 mm**

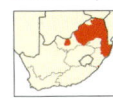

**HABITS** Weak fluttering flight in shade of forest canopy. Small groups perch together, slowly opening and closing their wings while sucking honeydew from scale insects. **HABITAT** Thickly wooded areas in savanna. **EARLY STAGES** Details not recorded. **VARIATION** Dark markings tend to be paler in dry season form (not shown). **SIMILAR SPECIES** Natal (p. 70) and Lipara (northern KZN, Maputaland) buffs have more intricately marked undersides. Natal Buff differs in being sexually dimorphic. Lipara told from Pennington's by its distribution, smaller size and darker colour. **STATUS** Scarce and local.

J F M A M J J A S O N D

## Amakosa Rocksitter
Amakoza-klipsitter
*Durbania amakosa*     **26–38 mm**

**HABITS** Weak fluttering flight. Quite sendentary; mostly rests on rocks. **HABITAT** Rocky grassy hillsides. **EARLY STAGES** *Egg* bun-shaped and ribbed. Black-brown. Laid singly on a rock. *Larva* up to 17 mm. Slug-shaped and hairy. Grey with black mottling. Feeds on lichen and cyanobacteria. *Pupa* up to 10 mm. Brownish-grey and hairy. Attached to old larval skin on sheltered side of a rock. **VARIATION** Sexually dimorphic, as shown. Slight colour variations among the seven subspecies (only *albescens*, *ayresi* and nominate shown here). **SIMILAR SPECIES** Natal Rocksitter (KZN, Mpu.) is smaller, darker and sexes similar; flies March–April. Clark's Rocksitter (E. and W. Cape) far smaller. Boland Rocksitter (W. and N. Cape) much darker with less finely marked underside. **STATUS** Locally common.

J F M A M J J A S O N D

## Southern Purple
**Suidelike-asvlerkie**
*Aslauga australis*      22–28 mm

**HABITS** Fluttering moth-like flight in the shade of trees. Only 20 records, so very little is known of its habits. This is probably South Africa's rarest butterfly. It is uncertain whether the species is endangered or just secretive. As related species further north are not rare, it remains a mystery as to why the species is as scarce as it is. **HABITAT** Coastal bush and savanna. **EARLY STAGES** Details not recorded. **VARIATION** Slight sexual dimorphism, as shown; female is paler and more grey than blue. **SIMILAR SPECIES** None. **STATUS** Rare.

J F M A M J J A S O N D

## Southern Pied Woolly Legs
**Suidelike bont-wolpootjie**
*Lachnocnema laches*      23–32 mm

**HABITS** Colonial. Flight rapid. Settles often. ♂ defends territory from a perch, or seen with ♀ sucking honeydew from scale insects. **HABITAT** Coastal bush and savanna. **EARLY STAGES** *Egg* disc-shaped. Pink. Laid singly or in pairs on grass stems or twigs near larval prey (*Hemipteran* sap suckers). *Larva* details unknown, but probably like Common Woolly Legs: up to 10 mm. Whitish-cream with grey-black patterns. Elongated 'true' legs adapted to seize prey. *Pupa* up to 8 mm. Rounded ends. Cream with red-brown markings. Forms on a leaf or bark. **VARIATION** Sexually dimorphic, as shown. **SIMILAR SPECIES** ♂ identical to Common Woolly Legs (E. Cape, Lim., Gau.), but ♀ of that species more evenly grey on upper side. D'Urban's Woolly Legs (E. Cape) is pale brown and occurs in grassland. **STATUS** Widespread but scarce.

J F M A M J J A S O N D

LYCAENIDAE: MILETINAE / SKOLLIES

## Boland Skolly
Boland-skollie
*Thestor protumnus*   22–42.5 mm

**HABITS** Colonial. Flight rapid. Often settles on the ground. ♂ defends territory. ♀ more sedentary. **HABITAT** Fynbos, succulent karoo and Nama karoo. **EARLY STAGES** *Egg* disc-shaped with prominent bulge. White, turning salmon. Laid singly or in small clusters on grass stems or twigs near *Hemipteran* larval prey. *Larva* up to 18 mm. Fat, oval, with small head. Cream-white. Full-grown larvae shelter with and are fed by *Anaplolepis* ants. *Pupa* up to 13 mm. Both ends rounded. Plain buff. Rests on floor of ants' nest. **VARIATION** ♂ has trident-shaped upper side forewing sex brand. Subspecies (not shown) *aridus* and *terblanchei* are paler bright, not deep dark, yellow. **SIMILAR SPECIES** 14 other 'yellow' buff to dun skollies occur in W., E. and N. Cape. Boland is most common and widespread. **STATUS** Locally common.

## Peninsula Skolly
Skiereiland-skollie
*Thestor yildizae*   25–39 mm

**HABITS** Colonial. Flight rapid. Often settles on the ground. ♂ defends territory. ♀ more sedentary. **HABITAT** Fynbos. **EARLY STAGES** *Egg* disc-shaped with prominent bulge on one side. White. Laid singly on grass stems or twigs close to nest of *Anaplolepis custodiens* ants. *Larva* up to 12 mm. Fat, oval with small head. Cream-white. Full-grown larva shelters in ants' nest and is fed by mouth. *Pupa* up to 12 mm. Both ends rounded. Plain buff. Formed on floor of ants' nest. **VARIATION** ♂ has trident-shaped upper side forewing sex brand. **SIMILAR SPECIES** 11 similar so-called 'black' skollies (actually dark grey to grey-brown) occur across W., E. and N. Cape provinces. Each species is geographically distinct. **STATUS** Locally common.

**LYCAENIDAE:** MILETINAE / SKOLLIES, SAPPHIRES

## Basuto Skolly
Basoetoe-skollie
*Thestor basutus*  30–42 mm

**HABITS** Colonial. Rapid, fluttering flight through grass. Settles on grass stems or the ground. ♂ defends territory; ♀ more sedentary. **HABITAT** Grassland and grassy areas in savanna. **EARLY STAGES** *Egg* disc-shaped with prominent bulge on one side. White. Laid singly or in small clusters on vegetation close to nest of *Anaplolepis custodiens* ants. *Larva* up to 16 mm. Fat and oval with small head. Cream-white. Full-grown larva shelters in ants' nest and is fed by mouth. *Pupa* up to 12 mm. Both ends rounded. Plain buff. Forms on floor of ants' nest. **VARIATION** ♂ has more triangular wings, while ♀ has more pronounced black-and-white markings on upper side forewing. Northern subspecies *capeneri* (not shown) is more conspicuously pied. **SIMILAR SPECIES** None. **STATUS** Locally common.

| J | F | M | A | M | J | J | A | S | O | N | D |

## Bowker's Marbled Sapphire
Bowker-se-marmersaffier
*Iolaus bowkeri*  26–41 mm

**HABITS** Low slow flight in thick bush. ♂ sometimes defends hill-top territory. **HABITAT** Karoo and savanna. **EARLY STAGES** *Egg* dimpled and domed. Laid singly on a leaf of *Viscum, Tapinanthus oleifolius* or *Ximenia*, depending on the subspecies. *Larva* up to 20 mm. Slug-like. Green. *Pupa* up to 13 mm. Green and brown. Attached to a leaf or to bark, where it is well camouflaged. **VARIATION** Sexes similar. Three similar subspecies: *I. b. bowkeri* (W. and E. Cape), *I. b. henningi* (FS, NW) and *I. b. tearei* (KZN, Mpu., Lim., Gau.). **SIMILAR SPECIES** Dusky Marbled Sapphire (N. Cape, northern Mpu.) is smaller with dark grey basal and discal areas on underside hind wing. **STATUS** Locally common and widespread.

| J | F | M | A | M | J | J | A | S | O | N | D |

LYCAENIDAE: THECLINAE / SAPPHIRES

## White-spotted Sapphire
Witkol-saffier
*Iolaus lulua*                      26–32 mm

**HABITS** Low flight in thick woodland. Shy and seldom seen. Occasionally found on flowers. **HABITAT** Sand and coastal forest. **EARLY STAGES** Few details recorded. *Larva* up to 18 mm. Variegated brown and cream. Feeds on the rare mistletoe *Oncocalyx bolusii*. **VARIATION** Sexes similar, but in ♂ blue patches on hind and forewings are not suffused with white; also has fewer and smaller white spots and shorter, more angular wings. **SIMILAR SPECIES** Upper side distinctive; underside resembles that of Purplebrown Hairstreak (p. 78), but the straight brown lines are broader. **STATUS** Very rare. Seldom seen, even at known haunts.

J F M A M J J A S O N D

## Southern Sapphire
Suidelike saffier
*Iolaus silas*                      32–41 mm

**HABITS** Rapid fluttering flight. ♂ flies high around tree tops and hill tops. ♀ found near food plants. **HABITAT** Nama karoo and lowland coastal forest. **EARLY STAGES** *Egg* dimpled and domed. White. Laid singly on a leaf of hairy mistletoe *Erianthemum dregei*. *Larva* up to 24 mm. Slug-like. Green. *Pupa* up to 15 mm. Berry-like. Green. Attached to leaves or bark. **VARIATION** Sexually dimorphic, as shown. **SIMILAR SPECIES** Straight-line Sapphire (KZN, Mpu., NW) has straighter red submarginal line on underside hind wing and ♂ upper side is duller blue. Trimen's Sapphire (Swa., Gau.,NW) has jagged black, not dark, red line on underside hind wing. **STATUS** Locally common.

J F M A M J J A S O N D

LYCAENIDAE: THECLINAE / SAPPHIRES

## Saffron Sapphire
**Geel-saffier**
*Iolaus pallene* — 30–38 mm

**HABITS** Flies quite slowly through thick vegetation, visiting flowers. Often hides among yellowed leaves. **HABITAT** Wooded savanna and open forest, often near to a river. **EARLY STAGES** *Egg* domed and faceted. Pale green. Laid singly or in pairs on a leaf of the edible sourplums *Ximenia caffra* or *X. americana*. *Larva* up to 20 mm. Slug-like. Bright green with white and pink shading. *Pupa* up to 15 mm. Resembles a broken twig. Buff with brown markings. Forms fixed to bark or twigs. Like all sapphires, the larva and pupa are superbly camouflaged. **VARIATION** Sexes identical. **SIMILAR SPECIES** None; this is the only yellow sapphire. **STATUS** Scarce but widespread.

| J | F | M | A | M | J | J | A | S | O | N | D |

## Red-line Sapphire
**Rooistreep-saffier**
*Iolaus sidus* — 28–33 mm

**HABITS** Rapid, fluttering flight. ♂ flies high around tree tops and hill tops. ♀ found near food plants. **HABITAT** Coastal forest, savanna and lowland coastal forest. **EARLY STAGES** *Egg* domed and dimpled. White, sometimes covered in a yellow film. Laid singly or in pairs on the leaf of a mistletoe in the Loranthaceae. *Larva* up to 15 mm. Has well-defined waist and a horn at tail end. Green and brown. *Pupa* up to 10 mm. Berry-shaped. Green and brown. Attached to leaves or bark. **VARIATION** Sexes differ, as shown. **SIMILAR SPECIES** Short-barred (KZN), Zimbabwe Yellow-banded (Lim., Zim.), Yellow-banded (E. Cape) and Natal Yellow-banded (p. 77) sapphires have three or four orange stripes on underside forewing, but Red-line Sapphire has only one red stripe there. **STATUS** Common.

| J | F | M | A | M | J | J | A | S | O | N | D |

## Mimosa Sapphire
**Doringboom-saffier**
*Iolaus mimosae*          **26–32 mm**

**HABITS** Low, fluttering flight among *Acacia* scrub. ♂ hill tops. Both sexes feed on flowers. **HABITAT** Nominate occurs in Nama karoo and savanna. Subspecies *rhodosense* occurs in savanna. **EARLY STAGES** *Egg* dimpled and domed. White. Laid singly or in pairs on a leaf of a mistletoe (Loranthaceae). *Larva* up to 20 mm. Slug-like. Green. *Pupa* up to 13 mm. Resembles broken twig. Typically whitish-grey to black, but may be any shade of pink or buff. Attached to leaves or bark. **VARIATION** Sexes similar. Subspecies *rhodosense* has paler blue upper side and plainer grey underside than nominate. **SIMILAR SPECIES** Smaller than other sapphires. Underside similar to that of Purplebrown Hairstreak (p. 78). **STATUS** Scarce but widespread.

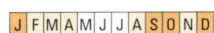

## Natal Yellow-banded Sapphire
**Natalsegeelstreep-saffier**
*Iolaus diametra natalica*      **26–29 mm**

**HABITS** Low fluttering flight. Settles on bushes. Strongly attracted to flowers. **HABITAT** Ranges from savanna to forest. **EARLY STAGES** *Egg* dimpled and domed. White. Laid singly on a flower or leaf of lighted matches, *Actinanthella wyliei*. *Larva* up to 16 mm. Slug-like. May be green, golden-yellow with russet stripes, or red. Well camouflaged on food plants. *Pupa* up to 13 mm. Resembles broken twig. Grey to brown, mottled with cream or pale green. Attached to a leaf or bark. **VARIATION** Sexually dimorphic. **SIMILAR SPECIES** Yellow-banded Sapphire (E. Cape) has single, not double, black marginal line at anal angle of underside hind wing. **STATUS** Scarce and local.

LYCAENIDAE: THECLINAE / HAIRSTREAKS

## Purplebrown Hairstreak
Persbruin-stertbloutjie
*Hypolycaena philippus philippus*     22–31 mm

**HABITS** Fast fluttering flight, low among thick scrub. Very fond of flowers. **HABITAT** Savanna, forest edges and coastal scrub. **EARLY STAGES** *Egg* dimpled and domed. White. Laid singly on a flower or leaf of one of many possible food plants. *Larva* up to 18 mm. Slug-like. Green. *Pupa* up to 10 mm. Smooth and oval with bulging abdomen. Grey-brown to bright green, depending on surroundings. Attached by a silk girdle to a leaf or bark. **VARIATION** Sexually dimorphic, as shown. **SIMILAR SPECIES** Coastal Hairstreak (Maputaland, KZN) almost identical, but postdiscal line of underside forewing bends sharply towards margin, a feature not easily seen on live specimens. **STATUS** Common and widespread.

| J | F | M | A | M | J | J | A | S | O | N | D |

## Buxton's Hairstreak
Buxton-se-stertbloutjie
*Hypolycaena buxtoni buxtoni*     25–33 mm

**HABITS** Fast fluttering flight. ♂ territorial, perching 2–4 m up and chasing intruders away; ♀ flies low along forest edges and streams. **HABITAT** Forest and coastal bush. **EARLY STAGES** Details not recorded. **VARIATION** Sexually dimorphic, as shown. **SIMILAR SPECIES** Purplebrown (above) and Coastal (Maputaland, KZN) hairstreak undersides grey; white underside may cause confusion with sapphires such as Southern Sapphire and similar species, but Buxton's is a smaller butterfly. **STATUS** Locally common.

| J | F | M | A | M | J | J | A | S | O | N | D |

## Azure Hairstreak
**Venda-se-stertbloutjie**
*Hemiolaus caeculus caeculus*  **30–38 mm**

**HABITS** Slow fluttering flight. Often occurs around low bushes, particularly food plants. **HABITAT** Savanna, riverine and coastal forest. **EARLY STAGES** *Egg* shape not recorded. Blue. Laid in small groups on flowers or leaves of *Olax dissitiflora* or *O. obtusifolia*. *Larva* size not recorded. Slug-like. Green. *Pupa* size not recorded. Similar to pupa of Purplebrown Hairstreak (p. 78). Forms among leaves of its food plant. **VARIATION** Sexually dimorphic, as shown. **SIMILAR SPECIES** Most sapphires have similarly bright blue upper sides, but Azure Hairstreak distinguished by unique deep red lines on underside hind wing. **STATUS** Locally common.

J F M A M J J A S O N D

## Tailed Black-eye
**Langstert-swartogie**
*Leptomyrina hirundo*  **19–26 mm**

**HABITS** Colonial. Low, weak, fluttering flight. Found near patches of its food plant. **HABITAT** Savanna, riverine and coastal forest and gardens. **EARLY STAGES** *Egg* a faceted dome. White. Laid singly on leaf of a *Cotyledon*, *Crassula*, *Kalanchoe* or *Bryophyllum* (all Crassulaceae). *Larva* up to 15 mm. Slug-like. Green. Lives inside a hollowed-out leaf of a succulent food plant. *Pupa* up to 9 mm. Rounded. Green to pale buff-pink. Forms inside a leaf or among leaf litter. **VARIATION** Sexes similar. **SIMILAR SPECIES** None. Its long hind wing tails are unique. Other black-eyes have brown, not steel blue, upper side. **STATUS** Locally common.

J F M A M J J A S O N D

## Common Black-eye
Gewone-swartogie
*Leptomyrina gorgias gorgias*  18–32 mm

**HABITS** Colonial. ♂ territorial, perching on low rocks and shrubs and chasing intruders away. Both sexes found near patches of favoured food plants. **HABITAT** Savanna and grassland. **EARLY STAGES** *Egg* a faceted dome. White. Laid singly on a leaf of a succulent in the Crassulaceae, like *Cotyledon*, *Crassula*, *Kalanchoe* or *Bryophyllum*. *Larva* up to 19 mm. Slug-like. Green. Lives inside hollowed-out leaf of food plant. *Pupa* up to 11 mm. Rounded. Green to brown, speckled with grey. Attached to a leaf or debris. **VARIATION** Sexes similar. **SIMILAR SPECIES** Henning's (western Lim., Gau., NW, N. Cape) and Cape (E., W., N. Cape) black-eyes similar, but ♂ in both cases lacks Common Black-eye's mauve-grey upper side scaling. Cape Black-eye has a bronze-brown sheen. **STATUS** Common and widespread.

J F M A M J J A S O N D

## Orange Banded Protea
Oranjeband-suikerbossie
*Capys alpheus*  31–47 mm

**HABITS** Very rapid flight. ♂ territorial, perching on low rocks and shrubs. ♀ flies around *Protea* bushes. **HABITAT** Fynbos, karoo vegetation and montane grassland. **EARLY STAGES** *Egg* domed, with finely netted surface texture. White. Laid singly on flower bud of a *Protea*. *Larva* up to 25 mm. Grub-like, covered in short bristles. Grey and buff. Lives inside hollowed-out bud, feeding on seeds. *Pupa* up to 15 mm. Rounded. Brown, speckled with black. Forms inside bud. **VARIATION** Sexes similar. In northern subspecies *extentus*, orange bands are broader than in nominate (not shown). **SIMILAR SPECIES** ♂ Russet Protea (p. 81) and Pennington's Protea (KZN, Drakensberg foothills) have narrower dark upper side margins. **STATUS** Locally common.

J F M A M J J A S O N D

# Russet Protea
**Sannie-se-suikerbossie**
*Capys disjunctus*

31–38 mm

**HABITS** ♂ flies fast and defends territory from a perch on a low rock or shrub. ♀ flies around *Protea* bushes. **HABITAT** Grassland with *Proteas*. **EARLY STAGES** *Egg* a large dome, with finely netted surface texture. White. Laid singly on the flower bud of a *Protea*. *Larva* up to 22 mm. Grub-like, covered in short bristles. Brownish-orange with blue markings. Lives inside hollowed-out bud, feeding on seeds. *Pupa* up to 14 mm. Rounded. Brown speckled with black. Forms inside a bud. **VARIATION** Sexually dimorphic, as shown. **SIMILAR SPECIES** Rare Pennington's Protea (KZN, Drakensberg foothills) both sexes similar; upper side paler bronze than ♂ Russet Protea. **STATUS** Locally common.

J F M A M J J A S O N D

# Orange-barred Playboy
**Skaduwee-spelertjie**
*Virachola diocles*

31–47 mm

**HABITS** ♂ flies fast and defends territory from a perch high up in a tree or shrub. ♀ flies lower and slower. Both sexes attracted to flowers. **HABITAT** Coastal and lowland forest and woodland. **EARLY STAGES** *Egg* domed with finely netted surface texture. Blue-green. Laid singly on a seed pod of one of many food plants, often *Bauhinia galpinii*. *Larva* up to 23 mm. Grub-like. Buff with black markings and russet front segments. Lives inside pods, feeding on seeds. *Pupa* up to 15 mm. Rounded. Brown speckled with black. Forms inside pod. **VARIATION** Sexually dimorphic, as shown. **SIMILAR SPECIES** Black-and-orange Playboy (KZN, Mpu., Lim.) is smaller and ♂ has totally black upper side forewing, while ♀ is darker than Orange-barred Playboy. **STATUS** Locally common.

J F M A M J J A S O N D

## Apricot Playboy
Oranje-spelertjie
*Virachola dinochares*      24–32 mm

**HABITS** Very rapid flight. ♂ territorial, flies high up, perching at the tops of trees and shrubs. ♀ flies lower. Both sexes attracted to flowers. **HABITAT** Savanna and thick woodland. **EARLY STAGES** *Egg* domed with finely netted surface texture. White or pale blue. Laid singly on a fruit of one of many food plants, often *Combretum zeyheri*. *Larva* up to 22 mm. Grub-like. Blue-grey to green with black markings. Lives inside pods, feeding on seeds. *Pupa* up to 13 mm. Rounded. Brown speckled with black. Forms inside pod. **VARIATION** Sexually dimorphic, as shown. **SIMILAR SPECIES** Orange Playboy (KZN, Maputaland) is larger and ♂ a more iridescent orange with darker upper side forewing tips; underside more heavily marked in both sexes. **STATUS** Common and widespread.

| J | F | M | A | M | J | J | A | S | O | N | D |

## Brown Playboy
Bruin-spelertjie
*Virachola antalus*      22–40 mm

**HABITS** Fast flight. ♂ territorial, perching on trees and shrubs; ♀ usually seen on flowers. **HABITAT** All biomes other than montane grassland. Quite rare in arid areas. **EARLY STAGES** *Egg* domed with finely netted surface texture. Pale green. Laid singly or in small groups on a fruit of one of a wide range of food plants, even the exotic *Cardiospermum grandiflorum*. *Larva* up to 20 mm. Grub-like. Varies from pale blue to red-brown or buff-grey with black markings. Lives inside pods, feeding on seeds. *Pupa* up to 13 mm. Rounded. Brown speckled with black. Forms inside pod. **VARIATION** Sexually dimorphic, as shown. **SIMILAR SPECIES** Van Son's Playboy (KZN, Lim., Swa.) is smaller and ♂ may have dull red triangle on upper side forewing, while ♀ lacks blue shading. **STATUS** Common and widespread.

| J | F | M | A | M | J | J | A | S | O | N | D |

## Common Fig-tree Blue
**Vyeboombloutjie**
*Myrina silenus*     **26–41 mm**

**HABITS** ♂ defends territory from a perch on a tree or shrub. Long tails give impression that it walks through the air. ♀ found near food plants. **HABITAT** Nominate occurs in grassland, savanna and forest. Subspecies *penningtoni* found in succulent karoo. **EARLY STAGES** *Egg* pill-shaped, large and faceted. White. Laid singly on a *Ficus* shoot. *Larva* up to 22 mm. Slug-like. Green with brown and white markings. *Pupa* up to 15 mm. Short and rounded. Brownish-green. Attached to leaf or debris. **VARIATION** Sexes similar. Subspecies *penningtoni* smaller and paler. **SIMILAR SPECIES** Lesser Fig-tree Blue (below) is smaller, shinier blue with brown upper side forewing tips, and occurs only in forest. **STATUS** Common and widespread.

## Lesser Fig-tree Blue
**Klein-vyeboombloutjie**
*Myrina dermaptera dermaptera*     **26–38 mm**

**HABITS** Keeps to forest canopy and seldom flies low. May swarm near suitable fig trees. Long tails give impression that it walks through the air. **HABITAT** Coastal and escarpment forest at lower altitudes. **EARLY STAGES** *Egg* pill-shaped, large and faceted. White. Laid singly or in small groups on a *Ficus* shoot. *Larva* up to 18 mm. Slug-like. Green with brown and white markings. *Pupa* up to 13 mm. Rounded, but more elongated than Common Fig-tree Blue. Buff, with brown and black mottling. Attached to bark, a dead leaf or debris. **VARIATION** Sexes similar. Winter specimens (not shown) have less blue. **SIMILAR SPECIES** Common Fig-tree Blue (above) not as shiny and has brown tips to upper side forewings. **STATUS** Scarce but widespread.

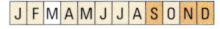

LYCAENIDAE: THECLINAE / HIGHFLIERS, BARS

## Hutchinson's Highflier
**Silwerrokkie**
*Aphnaeus hutchinsoni*      30–43 mm

**HABITS** ♂ defends hill-top territory, perching on trees and shrubs. ♀ found near food plants, but also on mud and flowers. **HABITAT** Savanna. **EARLY STAGES** *Egg* pill-shaped and dimpled. Grey. Laid singly or in small groups on a twig of *Burkea africana*, *Acacia robusta* or one of the Loranthaceae. *Larva* up to 30 mm. Slug-like. Grey with black markings. Attended by ants. *Larva* up to 30 mm. Green-brown when young and still feeding on leaves. Grey-brown mottled with black when fully grown. Details of food not recorded. *Pupa* up to 20 mm. Elongated. Brown with black speckling. Forms in a tunnel in bark. **VARIATION** Sexes similar. **SIMILAR SPECIES** None. **STATUS** Scarce but widespread.

J F M A M J J A **S O** N D

## Natal Bar
**Natalse-streepvlerkie**
*Cigaritis natalensis*      25–34 mm

**HABITS** ♂ defends hill-top territory from his perch. Both sexes attracted to mud and flowers. **HABITAT** Savanna, grassland and forest edges. **EARLY STAGES** *Egg* pill-shaped and dimpled. Chocolate brown. Laid singly on a shoot of, among others, *Canthium inerme*, *Clerodendrum glabrum*, *Ximenia caffra*. *Larva* up to 26 mm. Slug-like. White to grey with brown longitudinal markings. Attended by ants. *Pupa* up to 14 mm. Elongated. Brown speckled with black. Attached to bark or debris. **VARIATION** Sexes similar. Form *obscura* has wholly black upper side forewing tip. **SIMILAR SPECIES** Mozambique Bar (p. 85) more brightly coloured. Silvery (N. Cape to northern KZN) and Namaqua (N. Cape) bars have silver underside ground colour. Ella's Bar (N. Cape to northern KZN) is smaller and bars are not as straight. **STATUS** Common and widespread.

J F M A M J J A **S O** N D

## Mozambique Bar
**Mosambiek-streepvlerkie**
*Cigaritis mozambica*     **22–28 mm**

**HABITS** Colonial. Fast flight, close to ground, settling often on rocks or low vegetation. Both sexes confined to small areas, frequently on hill tops. **HABITAT** Savanna and grassland. **EARLY STAGES** Details not recorded, but larva known to feed on *Sphenostylis angustifolia*. **VARIATION** Sexes similar. **SIMILAR SPECIES** Natal Bar (p. 84) less brightly coloured. Silvery (N. Cape to northern KZN) and Namaqua (N. Cape) bars have silver underside ground colour. Ella's Bar (N. Cape to northern KZN) is duller with less regular underside markings. **STATUS** Locally common.

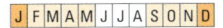

## Brilliant Gem
**Skitterjuweeltjie**
*Chloroselas pseudozeritis pseudozeritis*     **20–24 mm**

**HABITS** Colonial. Both sexes fly rapidly around the tops of large *Acacia* trees. Often seen feeding from flowers. **HABITAT** Savanna and lowland coastal bush. **EARLY STAGES** Details not recorded, but larval food plant likely to be an *Acacia*. **VARIATION** Sexually dimorphic, as shown. ♀ lacks blue flash on upper side. **SIMILAR SPECIES** Purple Gem (KZN, Mpu., Lim., Swa.) has grey-buff underside and more extensive violet, not green-blue, iridescence on upper side. **STATUS** Locally common.

## Eastern Scarlet
Ralie-rooivlerkie
*Axiocerses tjoane tjoane*          24–34 mm

**HABITS** Fast, low, buzzing flight. ♂ territorial. Perches in small bushes. Both sexes attracted to flowers. **HABITAT** Savanna, coastal bush and forest margins. **EARLY STAGES** *Egg* a smooth hemisphere. White. Laid in clusters on *Acacia* shoots. *Larva* up to 21 mm. Slug-shaped and hairy. Buff with brown markings. Gregarious. Lives in a bark crevice or in debris, attended by ants. *Pupa* up to 12 mm. Head blunt. Body tapers to tail. Brown-black. Forms in larval shelter. **VARIATION** Sexually dimorphic, as shown. Paler orange in arid areas. **SIMILAR SPECIES** Bush Scarlet (below). ♂ Dark-banded Scarlet (E. Cape, southern KZN) has black submarginal line on underside hind wing. ♂ Black-tipped Scarlet (northern KZN, Mpu., Lim., Gau., NW) has broader black upper side forewing tips. ♀ identical to ♀ Dark-banded and Black-tipped scarlets. **STATUS** Locally common.

| J | F | M | A | M | J | J | A | S | O | N | D |

## Bush Scarlet
Bos-rooivlerkie
*Axiocerses amanga amanga*          24–30 mm

**HABITS** Forms small colonies. Rapid low flight. ♂ perches in a small bush from which he defends territory. Both sexes attracted to flowers. **HABITAT** Savanna, coastal bush and forest margins. **EARLY STAGES** *Egg* a smooth hemisphere. White. Laid singly on a *Ximenia* leaf. *Larva* size not recorded. Slug-shaped and hairy. Green to brown with darker mottling. Lives in shelter attended by ants. *Pupa* size not recorded. Head blunt. Body tapers to tail. Black. Forms in larval shelter. **VARIATION** Sexes similar. **SIMILAR SPECIES** Dark-banded (E. Cape, southern KZN), Black-tipped (northern KZN, Mpu., Lim., Gau., NW) and Eastern (above) scarlets are sexually dimorphic and lack the silver-white costal blaze on underside forewing. **STATUS** Locally common.

| J | F | M | A | M | J | J | A | S | O | N | D |

LYCAENIDAE: THECLINAE / ARROWHEADS, COPPERS 87

## Silver Arrowhead
**Silwer-pylpuntjie**
*Phasis thero*  **31–47 mm**

♀

♀

**HABITS** Rapid evasive flight around small bushes and trees, near sand dunes, or along streams. **HABITAT** Fynbos. **EARLY STAGES** *Egg* domed with finely reticulated surface. Pinkish-grey. Laid singly on *Melianthus major* or a *Rhus*. *Larva* up to 30 mm. Flattened and slug-shaped. Dull green. Lives in a shelter attended by *Crematogaster peringueyi* ants. *Pupa* up to 20 mm. Slender. Blackish-brown. Forms in larval shelter. **VARIATION** Sexes similar, but ♂ darker. Subspecies *cedarbergae* (not shown) has squarer wings with better-defined, silver underside hind wing marks. **SIMILAR SPECIES** Three other arrowheads: the Namaqua (N., W. and eastern E. Cape) is darker, Brauer's (E. Cape) has more extensive orange and Pringle's (Sutherland area, N. Cape) has distinctive brown underside hind wing. **STATUS** Locally common.

## King Copper
**Koning-kopertjie**
*Tylopaedia sardonyx*  **32–50 mm**

♂

♀

**HABITS** Low rapid flight. ♂ defends hill-top territory from a perch on a rock or large bush. Both sexes regularly visit flowers, particularly vygies. **HABITAT** Rocky slopes and gullies in Nama karoo, succulent karoo and arid savanna. **EARLY STAGES** *Egg* domed, ribbed and covered in moles. Brown. Laid singly on *Aspalathus spinosa*, *Euclea undulata* or *Phylica oleaefolia*. *Larva* up to 25 mm. Flattened and slug-like. Brown to green. *Pupa* up to 20 mm. Elongated with rounded head and thorax. Brown. Forms under a rock. **VARIATION** Sexes similar, but ♂ has narrower wings. Subspecies *peringueyi* (W. Cape fynbos) (not shown) lacks white discal line on underside hind wing. **SIMILAR SPECIES** None. **STATUS** Locally common.

LYCAENIDAE: THECLINAE / COPPERS

## Warrior Silver-spotted Copper
Vegter-silwerkolkopertjie
*Argyraspodes argyraspis*     32–45 mm

**HABITS** Extremely fast flight. Settles frequently on low shrubs or on the ground, but remains wary. ♂ territorial. Both sexes visit flowers. **HABITAT** Nama and succulent karoo. **EARLY STAGES** Not recorded. **VARIATION** Sexes similar, but ♀ has broader wings. **SIMILAR SPECIES** Wallengren's (W. Cape), Wykeham's (N. and W. Cape, Large and McMasters' (N. to E. Cape) silver-spotted coppers and Scarce Mountain Copper (below) are smaller but also have silver-spotted underside hind wing. **STATUS** Locally common.

| J | F | M | A | M | J | J | A | S | O | N | D |

## Scarce Mountain Copper
Seldsame-bergkopertjie
*Trimenia malagrida*     24–33 mm

**HABITS** Low flight. Settles often on shrubs or the ground. ♂ territorial. Both sexes visit flowers. **HABITAT** Hillsides in dry fynbos. **EARLY STAGES** *Egg* domed and finely patterned with polygons. Covered in scales transferred from tip of ♀'s abdomen. Cream-white. Laid on twigs of plants near *Anaplolepis custodiens* ants. *Larva* up to 18.5 mm. Greenish-blue with uneven pinkish-maroon longitudinal stripes. Lives underground near ants' nest. *Pupa* up to 13 mm. Rounded. Yellowish-brown. Forms in hollows in soil. **VARIATION** Sexes similar, but ♂ has narrower wings. Four similar subspecies, among which is *maryae* (shown here). **SIMILAR SPECIES** Other silver-spotted coppers have more angular wings. **STATUS** *T. m. malagrida* and *T. m. paarlensis* threatened. Other subspecies under no threat but local and uncommon.

| J | F | M | A | M | J | J | A | S | O | N | D |

## Red Copper
Rooi-kopervlerkie
*Aloeides thyra*

22–28 mm

**HABITS** Small colonies. Flight low, fast, and erratic. Settles on the ground. ♀ wanders in search of laying sites.
**HABITAT** Fynbos and Nama karoo (sea level to altitude).
**EARLY STAGES** *Egg* details not recorded. Known to have been laid in sand near *Aspalathus* plants. *Larva* up to 24 mm. Grey-green with uneven reddish-brown longitudinal lines. Lives underground in nest of *Lepisiota capensis* ants. *Pupa* up to 14 mm. Rounded. Yellowish-brown. Forms in ants' nest. **VARIATION** Sexes similar, but ♂ has narrower wings. Underside ground colour varies from grey-brown to magenta red. **SIMILAR SPECIES** More than 20 *Aloeides* (rough coppers) are similar to Red Copper. **STATUS** Common and widespread.

J F M A M J J A S O N D

## Roodepoort Copper
Roodepoort-kopervlerkie
*Aloeides dentatis*

22–28 mm

**HABITS** Colonial. Low, fast, erratic flight. Usually settles on ground. ♀ wanders in search of egg-laying sites. **HABITAT** Montane and highveld grassland. **EARLY STAGES** *Egg* bun-shaped and finely cross-ribbed with tiny polygons. Cream-white, turning purple-brown. *Larva* up to 19 mm. Grey with uneven reddish-brown longitudinal lines. Lives underground in nest of *Lepisiota capensis* ants. *Pupa* up to 12 mm. Rounded. Yellowish-brown. Forms in ants' nest. **VARIATION** Sexes similar, but ♂ has narrower wings. Underside ground colour ranges from grey-brown to dark magenta. Subspecies *maseruna* (not shown) similar to nominate. **SIMILAR SPECIES** Genus *Aloeides* (rough coppers) is large with 12 species that have similarly toothed underside hind wing. **STATUS** Scarce and local. Nominate threatened.

J F M A M J J A S O N D

LYCAENIDAE: THECLINAE / ROUGH COPPERS

## Dusky Copper
**Dowwe-kopervlerkie**
*Aloeides taikosama*   22–33 mm

**HABITS** Colonial. Low, jerky, erratic flight. Usually settles on the ground. **HABITAT** Savanna and grassland. **EARLY STAGES** Not recorded. **VARIATION** Underside ground colour varies from pale buff to red-brown. ♂ has dark upper side with faint paler marks. ♀ has prominent orange markings. **SIMILAR SPECIES** In the rare Barbara's Copper (Kaapsehoop area, Mpu.) apical spot in underside forewing submarginal series is displaced towards margin. Dull (fynbos and karoo) and Trimen's (cool grassland) coppers lack small tails on hind wing. **STATUS** Scarce but widespread.

| J | F | M | A | M | J | J | A | S | O | N | D |

## Aranda Copper
**Aranda-kopervlerkie**
*Aloeides aranda*   20–31 mm

**HABITS** Colonial. Low, slow, erratic flight. Settles on the ground or low plants. **HABITAT** Savanna, wet Nama karoo and grassland. **EARLY STAGES** *Egg* a cross-hatched ribbed bun shape. Whitish. Laid singly or in pairs in sand below *Aspalathus* plants. *Larva* up to 18 mm. Cream-white with fine green longitudinal marks. Found close to the ground. *Pupa* up to 11 mm. Rounded. Pale green with whitish wing cases. **VARIATION** Sexes have similar markings, but ♂ has narrower wings. Underside ground colour grey-brown to magenta. Variable dark upper side marks. **SIMILAR SPECIES** Many similar rough coppers, but Aranda has small tail at anal angle of hind wing. **STATUS** Common and widespread.

| J | F | M | A | M | J | J | A | S | O | N | D |

**LYCAENIDAE: THECLINAE / DAISY COPPERS, OPALS**

# Donkey Daisy Copper
**Donkie-madeliefkopervlerkie**
*Chrysoritis zonarius*   18–24 mm

**HABITS** Found in dense colonies close to clumps of its food plant. Flight low, slow and fluttering. Settles frequently on low vegetation. **HABITAT** Coastal fynbos. **EARLY STAGES** Not recorded, but female lays eggs on *Chrysanthemoides incana* and larvae are associated with *Crematogaster peringueyi* cocktail ants. **VARIATION** Sexes similar. Subspecies *coetzeri* (Namaqualand) (not shown) is smaller and darker. **SIMILAR SPECIES** Jitterbug Daisy Copper (E. and W. Cape) and Feltham's Opal (W. and N. Cape) both occur in similar habitat, but are a far brighter shade of orange than Donkey Daisy Copper. **STATUS** Locally common.

| J | F | M | A | M | J | J | A | S | O | N | D |

# Natal Opal
**Natal-opaal**
*Chrysoritis natalensis*   24–34 mm

**HABITS** In colonies around clumps of its food plant. Flight rapid and circling, but brief. Settles on flowers and low vegetation. **HABITAT** Coastal bush, forest edges and savanna. **EARLY STAGES** *Egg* domed. White. Laid singly or in pairs on a shoot of *Chrysanthemoides monilifera* or *Cotyledon orbiculata*. *Larva* up to 20 mm. Flattened and rounded. Green with longitudinal brown stripes; rounded at both ends. Shelters with *Crematogaster lingmei* cocktail ants. *Pupa* up to 12 mm. Rounded. Black-brown. Forms in a small shelter attended by ants. **VARIATION** Sexes similar. **SIMILAR SPECIES** Eight other similar bright coppery opals with spotted wings occur through SA's karoo, grassland and fynbos habitats, but they lack the small tail at anal angle of hind wing. **STATUS** Locally common.

| J | F | M | A | M | J | J | A | S | O | N | D |

LYCAENIDAE: THECLINAE / OPALS

### Common Opal
Prag-opaal
*Chrysoritis thysbe*     24–35 mm

**HABITS** Fast, sustained flight. ♂ territorial on dunes and hilltops. ♀ found near food plants. **HABITAT** Coastal dunes and sandy areas in fynbos. **EARLY STAGES Egg** domed and cross-ribbed, creating tiny polygons. White. Singly or in pairs on *Chrysanthemoides monilifera*, a *Zygophyllum* or a *Thesium*. **Larva** up to 18 mm. Slug-shaped. Green with darker longitudinal stripes. In small shelters attended by *Crematogaster peringueyi* ants. **Pupa** up to 11 mm. Rounded. Black-brown. Forms in larval shelter. **VARIATION** Sexes similar. Seven similar subspecies; undersides may be marbled, like nominate, or plain, like *osbecki* shown here. **SIMILAR SPECIES** Over 20 species of small orange opal occur, all with a blue sheen. **STATUS** Locally common.

| J | F | M | A | M | J | J | A | S | O | N | D |

### Dark Opal
Bloujuweel-opaal
*Chrysoritis nigricans*     22–38 mm

**HABITS** Fast sustained flight. ♂ territorial. Perches in low vegetation. ♀ found near food plants. **HABITAT** Fynbos from just above sea level to high altitude (in the Zwartberg). **EARLY STAGES Egg** domed. White, turning brown. Laid singly or in pairs on an *Osteospermum*, *Zygophyllum* or *Thesium*. **Larva** up to 17 mm. Slug-shaped. Green. Shelters with *Crematogaster* cocktail ants. **Pupa** up to 9.5 mm. Rounded. Yellow-brown. Forms in larval shelter. **VARIATION** Sexually dimorphic, as shown. Subspecies *zwartbergae* is darker, while *rubrescens* (not shown) has broader red wing markings than nominate. **SIMILAR SPECIES** Uranus Opal (W. Cape) has less sharply angled forewings. ♂ Adonis Opal (W. Cape) has extensive red on upper side hind wing. **STATUS** Scarce and local.

| J | F | M | A | M | J | J | A | S | O | N | D |

LYCAENIDAE: THECLINAE / GREYS, SORREL COPPERS

## Silver-spotted Grey
Spikkel-valetjie
*Crudaria leroma*   20–34 mm

**HABITS** Found in colonies. Low, slow flight. Settles frequently. **HABITAT** Nama and succulent (not arid) karoo, as well as savanna and grassland. **EARLY STAGES Egg** domed and covered in scales transferred from ♀. White. Laid singly or in pairs on *Acacia karroo*, *A. sieberana* or *Elephantorrhiza burkei*. **Larva** up to 20 mm. Dull whitish with grey and red longitudinal stripes. Shelters with *Anaplolepis custodiens* pugnacious ants. **Pupa** up to 10 mm. Rounded. Yellow-brown. Forms in larval shelter. **VARIATION** Sexes similar, but length of small hind wing tails varies between populations. **SIMILAR SPECIES** Wykeham's and Cape greys (both in Nama karoo) very similar to Silver-spotted, separated only by genitalic dissection. **STATUS** Locally common.

J F M A M J J A S O N D

## Eastern Sorrel Copper
Oostelike-kleinkopervlerkie
*Lycaena clarki*   21–30 mm

**HABITS** Low, weak, intermittent flight. Settles often. Found near food plants. **HABITAT** Marshy areas in grassland, Nama and succulent karoo. **EARLY STAGES Egg** disc-shaped with a network of ribbing. White. Laid singly or in small clusters on a young shoot or flower of *Rumex lanceolatus*. **Larva** up to 16 mm. Slug-shaped. Varies from pale green to yellow-buff to pinkish-red. Lacks patterning. **Pupa** up to 10 mm. Rounded. Yellow-brown to green. Forms beneath a leaf. **VARIATION** Sexes similar. **SIMILAR SPECIES** Western Sorrel Copper (in fynbos) is smaller, scarcer, with less distinct pale grey spots on underside hind wing. **STATUS** Locally common.

J F M A M J J A S O N D

## Common Hairtail
**Donker-kortstertjie**
*Anthene definita*      21–29 mm

**HABITS** Rapid brief flight. ♂ fond of mud puddles. ♀ mostly seen on flowers. **HABITAT** Fynbos, karoo, savanna, forest and urban areas. **EARLY STAGES** *Egg* a finely cross-ribbed disc. Pale blue. Laid singly, often on one of the Fabaceae or Crassulaceae. *Larva* up to 15 mm. Slug-shaped with pointed dorsal processes. Green to red, or both. *Pupa* up to 10 mm. Rounded. Green to brown. Pale diamond-shaped dorsal mark. Fixed flat to a leaf or stem. **VARIATION** Sexually dimorphic, as shown. **SIMILAR SPECIES** Cupreous Hairtail (KZN to Gau. and Lim.) ♂ upper side pinkish-bronze. Pale and Millar's hairtails (eastern SA) upper side paler blue. Large Hairtail (KZN) underside rich brown. **STATUS** Common and widespread.

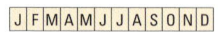

## Black Striped Hairtail
**Swartstreep-kortstertjie**
*Anthene amarah amarah*      21–29 mm

**HABITS** Fast whirling flight around flowering *Acacia* trees. ♂ territorial, but not on hill-tops. **HABITAT** Mainly thorny savanna. Also karoo and grassland areas where its food plants grow. **EARLY STAGES** *Egg* disc-shaped. White. Laid singly on an *Acacia* or related plant. *Larva* up to 17 mm. Slug-shaped with dorsal serrations. Green with darker green diagonal stripes. *Pupa* up to 12 mm. Rounded. Pale yellow to brown with faint, paler diagonal lines. Forms fixed to a leaf or bark. **VARIATION** Sexually dimorphic, as shown. **SIMILAR SPECIES** Otacilia, Talbot's and Little hairtails (which co-occur with Black Striped) and Mashuna Hairtail (p. 95) all have similar habits and underside markings, but lack broad black basal stripe on underside forewing. **STATUS** Common and widespread.

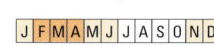

LYCAENIDAE: POLYOMMATINAE / HAIRTAILS

## Spotted Hairtail
Spikkel-kortstertjie
*Anthene larydas larydas*   26–29 mm

**HABITS** Fluttering flight at forest margins. ♂ territorial. ♀ often seen on flowers. Both sexes attracted to liquid and salts in mud. **HABITAT** Coastal forest and bush. **EARLY STAGES** *Egg* disc-shaped. Pale green. Laid singly on a young shoot of *Acacia kersteni*, *A. sieberana* or *Albizia adianthifolia*. *Larva* up to 15 mm. Slug-shaped with dorsal serrations. Green with darker green or reddish diagonal stripes. *Pupa* up to 10 mm. Rounded. Dull green with black dorsal line and pale diamond-shaped thoracic mark. Forms fixed to a leaf or bark. **VARIATION** Sexually dimorphic, as shown. **SIMILAR SPECIES** Very rare Juanita's Hairtail (Wolkberg, Lim.) lacks round dark spots at base of underside hind wing. **STATUS** Common and widespread.

J F M A M J J A S O N D

## Mashuna Hairtail
Mashuna-kortstertjie
*Anthene dulcis dulcis*   19–24 mm

**HABITS** Whirling buzzing flight around flowering *Acacia* trees. Feeds on low flowers. **HABITAT** Dry thorny savanna bush. **EARLY STAGES** Nothing published, but *Acacia karroo* and *A. tortilis* recorded as larval food plants. **VARIATION** Sexually dimorphic, as shown. ♀ impossible to separate in the field from two similar species. **SIMILAR SPECIES** Talbot's and Otacilia hairtails (same range as Black-striped Hairtail, p. 94) both have blue-violet upper side but former has no colour in area CuA1 or CuA2, while latter has colour in these as well as the cell and 1A + 2A (see wing diagram p. 5). **STATUS** Scarce but widespread.

J F M A M J J A S O N D

LYCAENIDAE: POLYOMMATINAE / HEARTS, BRONZES

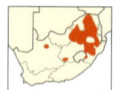

### Black Heart
**Swart-hartbloutjie**
*Uranothauma nubifer*     22–28 mm

**HABITS** Both sexes flutter around flowering *Acacia* trees. ♂ also attracted to water and salts in mud. **HABITAT** Moist *Acacia* savanna, especially near streams. **EARLY STAGES** *Egg* flattened and circular. White with boldly fluted edges. Laid on a shoot of *Acacia karroo*. *Larva* up to 14 mm. Slug-shaped with toothed dorsal ridge. Light brown with darker brown markings. *Pupa* up to 9 mm. Rounded. Black to brown. Forms on bark or a twig. **VARIATION** Sexually dimorphic, as shown. **SIMILAR SPECIES** None. **STATUS** Scarce but widespread.

| J | F | M | A | M | J | J | A | S | O | N | D |

### Bush Bronze
**Bos-malvabloutjie**
*Cacyreus lingeus*     22–28 mm

**HABITS** Slow low flight. Settles often on low plants. ♂ frequents mud puddles. **HABITAT** Forest, gardens, wooded savanna and stream banks. Absent from very arid areas. **EARLY STAGES** *Egg* circular and flattened. Green-white. Laid among the flower buds of a *Plectranthus* or another of the Lamiaceae. *Larva* up to 15 mm. Dorsal ridge double-toothed. Colour and patterns vary to match food plant. *Pupa* up to 9 mm. Hairy. Light brown with black speckling and double black dorsolateral stripes. **VARIATION** Sexually dimorphic, as shown. **SIMILAR SPECIES** In Mocker Bronze (Lowveld, northern SA) leading edge of costal spot on underside hind wing is angled away from body. **STATUS** Common and widespread.

| J | F | M | A | M | J | J | A | S | O | N | D |

## Common Geranium Bronze
**Malvabloutjie**
*Cacyreus marshalli* **15–27 mm**

**HABITS** Slow flight close to the ground. Stays near food plants. ♂ attracted to water and salts in mud puddles. **HABITAT** Absent only from the most arid areas. Favours gardens. **EARLY STAGES** *Egg* circular and flattened. Green-white. Laid among flower buds of one of the Geraniaceae. *Larva* up to 13 mm. Slug-like. Green to yellow with pink markings that vary in extent. *Pupa* up to 9 mm. Hairy. Green or yellow to brown with brown speckling. Forms hidden among leaf debris. **VARIATION** Sexes similar. **SIMILAR SPECIES** Water (eastern SA) and Dickson's geranium bronzes (W. to N. Cape coastal region) have similar undersides, but upper side sheen is violet in the former and metallic copper in the latter, not plain brown. **STATUS** Common and widespread.

## Hintza Pierrot
**Hintza-bloutjie**
*Zintha hintza* **24–27 mm**

**HABITS** Rapid flight. Stays close to the ground or near bushes. Both sexes fond of flowers. ♂ frequents mud puddles and defends territory from a prominent perch. **HABITAT** Thick savanna bush. **EARLY STAGES** *Egg* circular and flattened. White. Laid singly under the leaf of a *Ziziphus*. *Larva* up to 16 mm. Slug-like and flattened. Yellow-green with darker green markings. *Pupa* up to 10 mm. Slightly hairy. Dark brown with black speckling. Forms among leaf debris. **VARIATION** Sexually dimorphic, as shown. Subspecies *krooni* (arid N. Cape) has more extensive white upper side markings. **SIMILAR SPECIES** Black (p. 98) and White (northern SA Lowveld) pies have white underside with black spots, and no upper side blue. **STATUS** Scarce but widespread.

## Black Pie
**Swart-bontetjie**
*Tuxentius melaena*        19–25 mm

**HABITS** Rapid low flight. Fond of flowers and stays close to food plants. ♂ frequents mud puddles. **HABITAT** Savanna and coastal bush. **EARLY STAGES** *Egg* circular and flattened. White. Laid on a shoot of *Ziziphus mucronata* or *Z. zeyheriana*. *Larva* up to 12 mm. Slug-like and flattened. Yellow-green with red dorsal stripe. *Pupa* up to 8 mm. Slightly hairy. Cream with black speckling. Attached to a leaf or twig. **VARIATION** Sexes similar. Subspecies *griqua* (arid N. Cape and FS) (not shown) has fainter black underside spots and duller, more suffused black upper side. **SIMILAR SPECIES** White (E. Cape, Lim., NW) and Western (Orange River, N. Cape) pies. In former, white on upper side forewing reaches inner margin. In latter, dark upper side markings are a browner black and more extended. **STATUS** Widespread and common.

## Common Zebra Blue
**Gewone-ertjiebloutjie**
*Leptotes pirithous*        21–30 mm

**HABITS** Weak fluttering flight close to food plants. ♂ frequents mud puddles. **HABITAT** Common in gardens. **EARLY STAGES** *Egg* circular and flattened. White. Laid singly on a young shoot of a *Plumbago* or one of the Fabaceae. *Larva* up to 15 mm. Slug-like with toothed double dorsal ridge. Variable green to brown or red, depending on the food plant. *Pupa* up to 8 mm. Slightly hairy. Pale green to brown with black speckling. Attached to a concealed leaf or twig. **VARIATION** Sexually dimorphic, as shown. **SIMILAR SPECIES** Short-toothed (all SA, except central Karoo), Jeannel's, Babault's (northeastern SA) and Common Zebra blues can be separated only by genitalic dissection. Sesbania Blue (KZN) has suffused white at anal angle of upper side hind wing. **STATUS** Common and widespread.

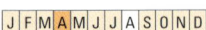

LYCAENIDA: POLYOMMATINAE / BLUES

## Pea Blue
**Lusern-bloutjie**
*Lampides boeticus*           24–34 mm

**HABITS** Strong sustained flight at about 1 m. ♂ competes for hill-top territory. Both sexes fond of flowers. **HABITAT** Very common in gardens. A pest where peas and beans grow. **EARLY STAGES** *Egg* circular and flattened. Dirty white. Laid singly on a bud or pod (Fabaceae). *Larva* up to 20 mm. Slug-like. Green to yellow or cream to match food plant with pink to brown diagonal markings. *Pupa* up to 13 mm. Brown with black markings. Attached to a hidden leaf or twig. **VARIATION** Sexually dimorphic, as shown. **SIMILAR SPECIES** Short-toothed (absent in central Karoo), Jeannel's, Babault's (northeastern SA) and Common Zebra (p. 98) blues smaller with less defined underside hind wing stripes. **STATUS** Widespread and common.

J F M A M J J A S O N D

## Vivid Dotted Blue
**Fynbos-spikkelbloutjie**
*Tarucus thespis*             20–27 mm

**HABITS** Fluttering flight among low vegetation. Settles frequently on prominent leaves and twigs. **HABITAT** Fynbos. **EARLY STAGES** *Egg* cup-shaped and covered with criss-cross ribbing and warts. White. Laid singly on a shoot of *Phylica imberbis*. Larva and pupa details not recorded. **VARIATION** Sexually dimorphic, as shown. **SIMILAR SPECIES** Dotted Blue (eastern and northern SA) occurs in grassland and savanna and has well-defined black spots on a white ground. Bowker's Blue (N. and E. Cape to Lim.) occurs in montane grassland and is larger with rounder, better-defined spots on upper side hind wing. **STATUS** Locally common.

J F M A M J J A S O N D

## Marsh Mountain Blue
Moeras-bergbloutjie
*Harpendyreus noquasa*   17–24 mm

**HABITS** Fluttering flight among low marsh vegetation. Settles frequently on prominent leaves and twigs. Both sexes fond of flowers. **HABITAT** Wet grassland in the foothills of the Drakensberg. **EARLY STAGES** Not recorded, but eggs laid on *Alchemilla capensis*. **VARIATION** Sexually dimorphic, as shown. **SIMILAR SPECIES** Tsomo Mountain Blue (E. Cape Drakensberg) has brown, not blue, on upper side in both sexes. Salvia Mountain Blue (Nama karoo) is larger with boldly chequered cilia. **STATUS** Locally common.

J F M A M J J A S O N D

## Dusky Lineblue
Donker-bloutjie
*Pseudonacaduba sichela sichela*   25–28 mm

**HABITS** High flight around tall trees. ♂ frequents mud puddles. Both sexes fond of flowers. **HABITAT** Forest and wooded savanna. **EARLY STAGES** Not recorded, but eggs laid on *Mundulea sericea*. **VARIATION** Sexually dimorphic, as shown. **SIMILAR SPECIES** Finely lined underside is unique among SA butterflies. **STATUS** Scarce but widespread.

J F M A M J J A S O N D

LYCAENIDAE: POLYOMMATINAE / BLUES

## Variable Blue
Verneuker-bloutjie
*Lepidochrysops variabilis*     28–37 mm

**HABITS** Strong rapid flight. Settles often. ♂ competes for hill-top territory. **HABITAT** Hilly country in grassland and fynbos vegetation. **EARLY STAGES** *Egg* a flattened sphere. Greenish-white. Laid on the ovaries of *Ocimum obovatum*, *Selago corymbosa* or *Salvia* flowers. *Larva* up to 18 mm. Slug-shaped. Pale whitish-cream. Young larva feeds on immature seeds, but from third instar feeds on the brood of *Camponotus niveosetosus* ants. *Pupa* length not recorded. Covered in short hairs. Brown. Forms in ants' nest. **VARIATION** Sexes similar. Variable spotting pattern on underside hind wing. KZN specimens may have blue scaling on upper side. **SIMILAR SPECIES** Genus *Lepidochrysops* includes 16 species of 'blues' with similar brown to black upper sides. Some are brown with a copper or bronze sheen. **STATUS** Locally common.

## Highveld Blue
Hoëveld-bloutjie
*Lepidochrysops praeterita*     36–44 mm

**HABITS** Colonial. Rapid, low, erratic flight. Remains close to food plants. **HABITAT** Grassy slopes among low hills. **EARLY STAGES** Details not recorded, but young larva known to feed on the ovaries of *Ocimum obovatum* flowers. Older larvae and pupae are found in ants' nests. **VARIATION** Sexually dimorphic, as shown. **SIMILAR SPECIES** Irving's (Mpu.) and Zulu (Mpu., Lim., Gau., NW, KZN) blues both have a similar brown underside, but told from Highveld Blue by brown, not blue, upper side. King (KZN, Mpu., Lim.) and Lotana (Lim.) blues distinguished by different underside patterning. **STATUS** Threatened.

### Peninsula Blue
Skiereiland-bloutjie
*Lepidochrysops oreas*      **24–38 mm**

**HABITS** Fast, erratic, sustained flight. ♂ competes for hill-top territory. ♀ stays close to food plants. **HABITAT** Mountain fynbos. **EARLY STAGES** *Egg* a flattened sphere. Blue-white. Laid on the ovaries of *Pseudoselago serrata* or *P. spuria* flowers. *Larva* details not fully recorded. Feeds on immature seeds initially, but on the brood of *Camponotus niveosetosus* ants when older. *Pupa* details not recorded, but forms in ants' nest. **VARIATION** Sexually dimorphic, as shown. Nominate subspecies *oreas* (Cape Peninsula) differs from subspecies *junae* (W. Cape hinterland) (not shown) in having wider dark upper side margins. **SIMILAR SPECIES** Genus *Lepidochrysops* includes 15 blues with varying shades of blue on the upper side. Some females have far less blue or are plain brown. **STATUS** Locally common.

### Twin-spot Blue
Dubbelkol-bloutjie
*Lepidochrysops plebeia plebeia*      **35–45 mm**

**HABITS** Rapid flight. Perches on bushes or rocks. ♂ competes for hill-top territory. ♀ stays in the shade of thorn trees close to food plants. **HABITAT** Hilly savanna. **EARLY STAGES** *Egg* a flattened sphere. Blue-white. Laid in clumps of 2–5 at a time on the ovaries of *Lantana rugosa* flowers. *Larva* size not recorded. Cream with reddish markings when young. Older larva details not recorded. Feeds on immature seeds initially, but from third instar on the brood of *Camponotus* ants. *Pupa* details not recorded. Probably forms in ants' nest. **VARIATION** Sexually dimorphic, as shown. **SIMILAR SPECIES** Free State Blue (E. Cape to Gau., NW) has similar grey-brown upper and under sides, but is a smaller, colonial species. **STATUS** Scarce but widespread.

LYCAENIDAE: POLYOMMATINAE / ANT BLUES

## Patricia Blue
Patricia-bloutjie
*Lepidochrysops patricia*    35–46 mm

**HABITS** Fast, low, sustained flight. ♀ stays near food plants. **HABITAT** Grassland and savanna. **EARLY STAGES** *Egg* a flattened sphere. Blue-white. Laid singly on the ovaries of *Lantana rugosa*, *L. camara* or *Salvia repens* flowers. *Larva* up to 20 mm. Slug-shaped. Pale flesh colour. Feeds on immature seeds initially, but from third instar on the brood of *Camponotus maculatus* ants. *Pupa* up to 14 mm. Rounded. Forms in ants' nest. **VARIATION** Sexually dimorphic, as shown. **SIMILAR SPECIES** Rossouw's (Mpu.) and Silvery (KZN to NW, Lim.) blues have silver-blue upper side. In Rossouw's this is suffused with grey. **STATUS** Common and widespread.

| J | F | M | A | M | J | J | A | S | O | N | D |

## Brilliant Blue
Helder-bloutjie
*Lepidochrysops asteris*    32–44 mm

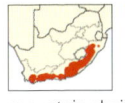

**HABITS** Fast sustained flight. ♂ flies along hillside contours. ♀ stays near food plants. **HABITAT** Fynbos and grassland along mountain chains. **EARLY STAGES** *Egg* a flattened sphere. White. Laid singly on the ovaries of *Ocimum burchellianum*, *Plectranthus grandidentatus* or *Pseudoselago serrata* flowers. *Larva* details not recorded, but young larva known to feed on immature seeds, and older larva presumed to feed on the brood of *Camponotus* ants. *Pupa* details not recorded, but probably forms in ants' nest. **VARIATION** Sexually dimorphic, as shown. **SIMILAR SPECIES** Swanepoel's (Mpu.) and Graham's (E. Cape) blues are smaller with well-marked undersides and duller blue upper sides. Trimen's Blue (W. Cape) same size, but with much darker blue upper side. **STATUS** Locally common.

| J | F | M | A | M | J | J | A | S | O | N | D |

## Brenton Blue
Brenton-bloutjie
*Orachrysops niobe*      24–42 mm

**HABITS** Colonial. Low fast flight. Settles often on the ground or in low vegetation. **HABITAT** Sandy coastal fynbos. **EARLY STAGES** *Egg* disc-shaped. White. Laid singly under a leaf of *Indigofera erecta*. *Larva* up to 19 mm. Slug-shaped. Cream. Young larva feeds on leaf surface. Older larva eats roots. *Pupa* up to 13.5 mm. Rounded. Buff-brown. Associated with *Camponotus baynei* ants. **VARIATION** Sexually dimorphic, as shown. **SIMILAR SPECIES** Karkloof Blue (below) has more contrasting underside. Grizzled Blue (p. 105) is *on average* smaller and duller. Of the nine similar *Orachrysops* blues, the closest is Brinkman's Blue (Kammanassie range, W. Cape), which is separated by teardrop shape of black spots on underside forewing. **STATUS** Threatened.

J F M A M J J A S O N D

## Karkloof Blue
Karkloof-bloutjie
*Orachrysops ariadne*      26–40 mm

**HABITS** Colonial. ♂ flight rapid, patrolling. Prefers to settle on dead plants. ♀ flight slower, near to food plants. **HABITAT** Mistbelt grassland. **EARLY STAGES** *Egg* disc-shaped with fine cross-ribbing. Pale green. Laid singly or in a small group under a leaf of *Indigofera woodii*. *Larva* up to 15 mm. Slug-shaped. Yellow-green. Feeds on leaf surface initially; probably on the roots of its food plant later. *Pupa* up to 15 mm. Rounded. Cream-yellow to brown. Associated with *Camponotus natalensis* ants. **VARIATION** Sexually dimorphic, as shown. **SIMILAR SPECIES** There are 11 similar blues in *Orachrysops*: Brenton Blue (above) has flatter grey underside. Grizzled Blue (p. 105) is *on average* smaller and duller. Of remainder, closest is Royal Blue (Lim.), but its undersides are a far paler grey. **STATUS** Threatened.

J F M A M J J A S O N D

LYCAENIDAE: POLYOMMATINAE / ANT BLUES, BLUES

## Grizzled Blue
Grou-bloutjie
*Orachrysops subravus*  30–36 mm

♂

**HABITS** Occurs in large colonies. Fast, low, wandering flight, up and down hillsides. **HABITAT** Grassy slopes in montane grassland. **EARLY STAGES** *Egg* disc-shaped. Green. Laid singly or in small groups under a leaf of *Indigofera tristis* or *I. woodii*. *Larva* feeds on leaf surface when young and thought to be associated with *Camponotus* ants later, but no further details available. *Pupa* details not recorded. **VARIATION** Sexually dimorphic, as shown. **SIMILAR SPECIES** There are 11 similar blues in *Orachrysops*, including the Brenton (p. 104) and Karkloof (p. 104) blues, which are larger and rarer. The remaining eight are not shown. **STATUS** Locally common.

♀

♀

J F M A M J J A S O N D

## Common Smoky Blue
Gewone-dowwebloutjie
*Euchrysops malathana*  22–31 mm

♂

**HABITS** Slow wandering flight among vegetation. **HABITAT** Savanna and grassy areas in savanna. **EARLY STAGES** *Egg* disc-shaped. Pale green. Laid in small groups on a flower stalk of one of the Fabaceae, such as a *Vigna* or on lucerne *Medicago sativa*. *Larva* up to 13 mm. Slug-shaped. Green with reddish diagonal marks. Feeds on flower ovaries, attended by ants. *Pupa* up to 10 mm. Rounded. Greenish-grey to yellow-brown with small black spots. Forms under a leaf. **VARIATION** Sexually dimorphic, as shown. **SIMILAR SPECIES** ♂ is only *Euchrysops* with grey upper side. ♀ resembles Osiris and Barker's smoky blues (E. Cape to Lim.) but is tailless. **STATUS** Common and widespread.

♀

J F M A M J J A S O N D

### Ashen Smoky Blue
Asvaal-dowwebloutjie
*Euchrysops subpallida*     23–28 mm

**HABITS** Colonial. Low weak flight. Both sexes fond of flowers. ♂ frequents mud puddles. **HABITAT** Savanna and grassy areas within savanna. **EARLY STAGES** Details not recorded, although larval food plants belong to genus *Ocimum*. **VARIATION** Sexually dimorphic, as shown. **SIMILAR SPECIES** Sabie Smoky Blue (E. Cape to Lim. and NW) has dull grey underside. Smaller than Osiris and Barker's smoky blues (E. Cape to Lim.). **STATUS** Common and widespread.

### Cupreous Blue
Koperbloutjie
*Eicochrysops messapus*     17–24 mm

**HABITS** Flight low and weak. Fond of flowers. ♂ frequents mud puddles. **HABITAT** Savanna, karoo, grassland and fynbos. Absent from only the most arid areas. **EARLY STAGES** *Egg* disc-shaped. Pale blue. Laid singly on a *Thesium*. *Larva* up to 10 mm. Elongated and slug-shaped. Green. Feeds on buds and flowers. *Pupa* up to 8 mm. Elongated with long white hairs. Green. Forms on a leaf or stem. **VARIATION** Sexually dimorphic, as shown. ♂ of nominate subspecies (W., E. and N. Cape) (not shown), which overlaps with *mahallokoeana* in FS, lacks pink-copper patch on upper side forewing. **SIMILAR SPECIES** Resembles many other small blues, but separated by single large anal lunule on upper side hind wing and by sparse black spots on underside. **STATUS** Common and widespread.

LYCAENIDAE: POLYOMMATINAE / ANT BLUES

## White-tipped Blue
**Witpunt-koperbloutjie**
*Eicochrysops hippocrates*      **18–24 mm**

**HABITS** Colonial. Low weak flight. Both sexes fond of flowers. ♂ territorial and frequents mud puddles. **HABITAT** Near water in forest, savanna and coastal bush. **EARLY STAGES Egg** disc-shaped. Pale green. Laid singly on *Persicaria setulosa* or a *Rumex*. **Larva** up to 12 mm. Slug-shaped and elongated. Green to pink, depending on food. Feeds on leaves and flowers. **Pupa** up to 8 mm. Elongated and covered in short hairs. Pale buff, finely speckled with grey. Forms on a leaf or stem. **VARIATION** Sexually dimorphic, as shown. **SIMILAR SPECIES** ♂ unique. ♀ resembles many other small blues, but distinguished by pale underside with sparse black spotting. **STATUS** Locally common.

J F **M A M** J J A S O N D

## Common Meadow Blue
**Vleibloutjie**
*Cupidopsis cissus cissus*      **22–36 mm**

**HABITS** Low flight that may be sustained. Fond of flowers. ♂ frequents mud puddles. **HABITAT** Savanna and grassland. **EARLY STAGES Egg** disc-shaped. White. Laid singly on an *Eriosema*, *Rhynchosia* or *Vigna* flower bud. **Larva** up to 18 mm. Slug-shaped. Green with green and white stripes, or white with red and pink stripes. Feeds on flowers and seeds. **Pupa** up to 10 mm. Narrow. Green with black dorsal line. Covered in white hairs. Forms on a leaf or stem. **VARIATION** Sexually dimorphic, as shown. **SIMILAR SPECIES** Superficially resembles a *Lepidochrysops* blue on the wing, but underside differs. Tailed Meadow Blue (similar range) has short tail on each hind wing. **STATUS** Common and widespread.

J F M A M **J J A S** O N D

## Rayed Blue
**Witstreep-bloutjie**
*Actizera lucida* — 15–25 mm

**HABITS** Weak flight, close to the ground. Settles often on grass. **HABITAT** Grassland and grassy savanna. **EARLY STAGES** *Egg* disc-shaped. Pale blue-green. Laid singly on an *Argyrolobium*, *Rhynchosia*, *Crotolaria*, *Oxalis* or *Vigna* flower bud. *Larva* up to 12 mm. Slug-shaped. Green to white with diagonal stripes matching flower colour of food plant. Feeds on flowers and seeds. *Pupa* up to 8 mm. Pale green-yellow to grey-brown to match surroundings. Forms on a leaf or stem. **VARIATION** Sexually dimorphic, as shown. **SIMILAR SPECIES** Rare Red-clover Blue (E. Cape, Les., southern FS) lacks the unique white diagonal stripe on underside hind wing and sexes are similar, not dimorphic, with white upper side spots on a black ground. **STATUS** Common and widespread.

| J | F | M | A | M | J | J | A | S | O | N | D |

---

## African Grass Blue
**Duwweltjie-bloutjie**
*Zizeeria knysna knysna* — 18–26 mm

**HABITS** Slow flight near the ground. Visits lawns, flower beds and waste ground. **HABITAT** Most open grassy areas; common in gardens. **EARLY STAGES** *Egg* a flattened sphere. Pale blue-green. Laid singly on a leaf or bud of low-growing plants like *Oxalis corniculata* or *Tribulus terrestris*. *Larva* up to 11 mm. Slug-shaped. Pale whitish to grey-green with whitish diagonal stripes and dorsal line. Feeds on leaves and flowers. *Pupa* up to 8 mm. Pale yellow to green with variable grey markings. Forms in plant debris. **VARIATION** Sexually dimorphic, as shown. **SIMILAR SPECIES** Tiny Grass Blue (p. 111) has more elongated abdomen. Rayed Blue (above) has diagonal white stripe on underside hind wing. Dark Grass Blue (eastern SA) has a kink in the series of discal spots on underside hind wing. **STATUS** Common and widespread.

| J | F | M | A | M | J | J | A | S | O | N | D |

LYCAENIDAE: POLYOMMATINAE / DWARF BLUES, BABUL BLUES

## Dwarf Blue
**Dwerg-bloutjie**
*Oraidium barberae*            10–18 mm

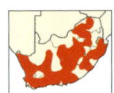

**HABITS** Slow flight, close to the ground. ♂ defends small territory among rocks or low vegetation. **HABITAT** Braod habitat from forest to arid savanna, but needs short grass and patches of sand. **EARLY STAGES** *Egg* Details not recorded. *Larva* up to 10 mm. Slug-shaped, finely bristled, with dorsal humps. Pale green with faint longitudinal pink-mauve lines. Feeds on *Crassula expansa fragilis*. *Pupa* up to 8 mm. Elongated and hairless, with rounded ends. Pale green. Forms among leaves or flowers of food plant. **VARIATION** Sexes similar. **SIMILAR SPECIES** Tinktinkie Blue (E., W. and N. Cape, FS, KZN), which shares with Dwarf Blue the status of SA's smallest butterfly. The latter has buff streaks at anal angle (see arrow) and white markings around the grey spots on underside hind wing. **STATUS** Scarce but widespread.

J F M A M J J A S O N D

## Topaz Babul Blue
**Hemels-bloutjie**
*Azanus jesous*            17–28 mm

**HABITS** Rapid fluttering flight. Usually at the crown of a flowering *Acacia*. ♂ frequents mud puddles. **HABITAT** Savanna, succulent and Nama karoo with *Acacia* trees. **EARLY STAGES** *Egg* a flattened sphere. Pale green-white. Laid singly on an *Acacia* or *Dichrostachys* shoot or bud. *Larva* up to 12 mm. Slug-shaped with ridged back. Green with whitish diagonal stripes and red dorsal line. *Pupa* up to 9 mm. Pale green with variable grey markings. Forms among leaves. **VARIATION** Sexually dimorphic, as shown. **SIMILAR SPECIES** Natal (p. 110), Black-bordered (p. 110), Velvet-spotted (throughout SA) and Pale (E. Cape to Gau. and Lim.) babul blues. ♂ separated from these similar species by pinkish tone of ground colour and extensive brown bands on underside forewing. ♀ easier to distinguish. **STATUS** Common and widespread.

J F M A M J J A S O N D

LYCAENIDAE: POLYOMMATINAE / BABUL BLUES

## Natal Babul Blue
Natalse-bloutjie
*Azanus natalensis*  28–30 mm

**HABITS** Slower and lower flight than other *Azanus* blues. ♂ frequents mud puddles. **HABITAT** Moist savanna. **EARLY STAGES** *Egg* a flattened sphere. White. Laid singly on a young shoot or bud of *Acacia karroo* or *A. sieberana*. *Larva* up to 12 mm. Slug-shaped with ridged back. Green with whitish diagonal stripes and brown dorsal line. *Pupa* up to 8 mm. Pale green with variable grey markings. Forms among leaves. **VARIATION** Sexually dimorphic, as shown. **SIMILAR SPECIES** The largest *Azanus* blue. Black-bordered (below) and Pale (E. Cape to Gau. and Lim.) babul blues have discal spot on costa that is closer to wing margin than that next to it. In Natal Babul Blue discal spot is closer to wing base (see arrow). **STATUS** Scarce but widespread.

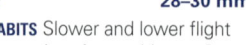

## Black-bordered Babul Blue
Doringboom-bloutjie
*Azanus moriqua*  19–25 mm

**HABITS** Rapid fluttering flight. Fond of flowers. Usually seen at the crown of a flowering *Acacia*. ♂ frequents mud puddles. **HABITAT** Mainly savanna. Scarce in karoo vegetation. **EARLY STAGES** *Egg* a flattened sphere. Green. Laid singly on a young shoot or bud of *Acacia karroo* or an *Entada*. *Larva* up to 10 mm. Slug-shaped with ridged back. Green with variable brown, pink or white markings. *Pupa* up to 8 mm. Dull yellow-green with variable grey markings. Forms among leaves. **VARIATION** Sexually dimorphic, as shown. **SIMILAR SPECIES** Pale Babul Blue (E. Cape to Gau., Lim.) has orange lunule next to black anal spot. **STATUS** Common and widespread.

# Grass Jewel
Grasjuweeltjie
*Chilades trochylus*     **17–25 mm**

**HABITS** Low rapid flight. Settles often on bare earth. Both sexes fond of flowers. ♂ frequents mud puddles. **HABITAT** Grassland and grassy savanna in all provinces, but absent from very arid areas. **EARLY STAGES Egg** a flattened sphere. Pale green. Laid singly on a young shoot of an *Indigofera* or *Heliotropium*. **Larva** up to 8 mm. Slug-shaped. Green to red with variable dark green, pink or red diagonal marks. **Pupa** up to 7 mm. Rounded. Dull yellow-green with buff wing cases. **VARIATION** Sexes similar. **SIMILAR SPECIES** Resembles ♀ Cupreous Blue (p. 106) but has more white-ringed dark spots on underside and always has three gold-ringed black spots at anal angle of hind wing. **STATUS** Scarce but widespread.

J F M A M J J A S O N D

# Tiny Grass Blue
Gaika-bloutjie
*Zizula hylax*     **17–25 mm**

**HABITS** Low, feeble, fluttering flight, close to food plants. Settles often, slowly waggling its wings from side-to-side. **HABITAT** Grassland and grassy areas. Penetrates arid regions along rivers. **EARLY STAGES Egg** disc-shaped. White. Laid singly on a member of the Acanthaceae such as *Phaulopsis imbricata*, *Chaetacanthus setiger*, *Justicia*, *Dyschoriste* or *Ruellia*, but may also be laid on *Oxalis corniculata* or *Tribulus terrestris*. **Larva** up to 9 mm. Slug-shaped. Green with dark green or red diagonal markings to a variable extent. **Pupa** up to 7 mm. Narrow. Dull yellow-green with short white hairs. **VARIATION** Sexually dimorphic, as shown. **SIMILAR SPECIES** African Grass Blue (p. 108) larger with shorter, more rounded wings. Never waggles its wings. **STATUS** Common.

J F M A M J J A S O N D

## African Clouded Yellow

Lusernskoenlapper
*Colias electo electo* 35–40 mm

**HABITS** ♂ flight fast, erratic and low. ♀ flies slower, staying close to food plants. **HABITAT** Grassy areas all over SA, but especially common on farms where lucerne is grown. **EARLY STAGES Egg** an elongated oval. Salmon pink with yellow top. Laid singly on one of the Fabaceae, such as *Medicago sativa* or a *Trifolium*. **Larva** up to 30 mm. Tapers to the tail. Green with minute black spots. Yellow lateral and dark green dorsal stripes. **Pupa** up to 23 mm. A narrow oval, pointed at both ends. Pale green with black or white lateral lines. Hangs from a leaf or stem by the tail and a silk midriff girdle. **VARIATION** Sexually dimorphic, as shown. Two ♀ forms – the nominate and a white form *aurivillius* (not shown). **SIMILAR SPECIES** None. **STATUS** Common and widespread.

| J | F | M | A | M | J | J | A | S | O | N | D |

## African Migrant

Afrikaanse swerwer
*Catopsilia florella* 54–66 mm

**HABITS** Strong sustained flight. May swarm. ♂ frequents mud puddles. **HABITAT** Most common in savanna areas where its food plants grow. **EARLY STAGES Egg** an elongated vertically fluted oval. Yellow-white. Laid on a member of the Fabaceae, such as a *Cassia*, *Senna* or *Chamaecrista*. **Larva** up to 47 mm. Cylindrical; tapers to tail. Green with tiny black spots and yellow and black lateral stripes. **Pupa** up to 32 mm. A narrow oval, with pointed ends. Pale green with white shading. Hangs from a leaf or stem by the tail and a silk midriff girdle. **VARIATION** Sexually dimorphic, as shown. Three ♀ forms – the nominate (shown), a male-like form *pyrene* and a yellow-white form *hyblaea*. **SIMILAR SPECIES** ♂ Large Vagrant (p. 115) has black upper side forewing tips. **STATUS** Common and widespread.

| J | F | M | A | M | J | J | A | S | O | N | D |

PIERIDAE: COLIADINAE / GRASS YELLOWS, PIERINAE / ZEBRA WHITES 113

# Broad-bordered Grass Yellow
Grasveldgeletjie
*Eurema brigitta brigitta*     30–35 mm

**HABITS** Low wandering flight close to the ground. ♂ frequents mud puddles. **HABITAT** Grassland and savanna. **EARLY STAGES** *Egg* an elongated oval. Yellow-white. Laid on *Chamaecrista mimosoides*. *Larva* up to 20 mm. Cylindrical, tapering towards tail. Green with yellow and dark green lateral stripes and green to red dorsal stripe. *Pupa* up to 18 mm. Elongated and elliptical with pointed ends. Pale green with variable dark speckling. Hangs from a plant by the tail and a silk midriff girdle. **VARIATION** Sexually dimorphic, ♀ is a paler, greener yellow. Nominate dry season form is paler than wet season form *zoe* with a pink underside hind wing. **SIMILAR SPECIES** Lowveld Yellow (E. Cape to Lim.) is larger with lobed upper side forewing tips. Angled Grass Yellow (same range) has squared hind wing edge. **STATUS** Common and widespread.

# Zebra White
Quagga
*Pinacopteryx eriphia eriphia*     40–47 mm

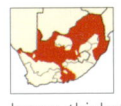

**HABITS** Fast wandering flight, close to the ground. Fond of flowers. ♂ frequents mud puddles. **HABITAT** Grassland, karoo, thicket and savanna. Absent only from very arid karoo and cold grassland areas. **EARLY STAGES** *Egg* an elongated oval. Yellow. Laid in clusters on a *Boscia*, *Cadaba* or *Maerua*. *Larva* up to about 25 mm. Grey-brown with lateral rows of brown-edged yellow stripes and pale elliptical spots. A fringe of hairs helps to reduce its shadow. *Pupa* up to 20 mm. Very elongated. Both ends pointed. Greyish-buff. Hangs from a leaf or stem by the tail and a silk midriff girdle. **VARIATION** Sexes similar. Dry season specimens cream, not white. **SIMILAR SPECIES** ♀ Smoky Orange Tip (p. 120) may be as dark, but has orange wing tips. **STATUS** Scarce but widespread.

## Vine-leaf Vagrant
Druiweblaarswerwer
*Eronia cleodora*        45–62 mm

**HABITS** Fast, random, wandering flight at or above head height. Fond of flowers. **HABITAT** Coastal bush, forest and moist savanna. **EARLY STAGES** *Egg* an elongated fluted oval. Pale yellow. Laid singly on a shoot of *Capparis fascicularis*, *C. tomentosa* or a *Salvadora*. *Larva* up to 36 mm. Cylindrical. Bright green with tiny yellow warts and cream lateral stripes. *Pupa* up to 30 mm. Laterally fattened. The greatly expanded wing cases form a semicircular keel. Green. Hangs from a leaf or stem by the tail and a silk midriff girdle. **VARIATION** Sexes similar. Dry season forms (top image) have narrower black borders on upper side. **SIMILAR SPECIES** None. **STATUS** Common and widespread.

## Autumn-leaf Vagrant
Herfblaarswerwer
*Afrodryas leda*        50–56 mm

**HABITS** Very rapid direct flight at or above head height. Settles briefly on flowers. **HABITAT** Coastal bush and forest, as well as moist savanna along the escarpment. **EARLY STAGES** *Egg* an elongated fluted oval. Pale yellow. Laid singly on the edge of a *Capparis* or *Cadaba* leaf. *Larva* up to 35 mm. Cylindrical. Dull leaf green with tiny yellow warts and a cream lateral stripe. *Pupa* up to 30 mm. Flattened laterally with greatly expanded wing cases that form a semicircular keel frontally. Green. Hangs from a leaf or stem by the tail and a silk midriff girdle. **VARIATION** Sexually dimorphic, as shown. Wet season specimens (not shown) have heavier dark markings. **SIMILAR SPECIES** None. **STATUS** Scarce but widespread.

PIERIDAE: PIERINAE / VAGRANTS

## Large Vagrant
Groot swerwer
*Nepheronia argia*      **50–70 mm**

**HABITS** ♂ flight very fast and direct, at or above head height. ♀ flies slower, staying near food plants. **HABITAT** Coastal bush and forest. **EARLY STAGES** *Egg* an elongated fluted oval. Pale cream. Laid singly on *Hippocratea longipetiolata*. *Larva* up to 45 mm. Cylindrical. Deep green with brown lateral blotches. *Pupa* up to 32 mm. Flattened laterally with wing cases forming a semicircular frontal keel. Pale green dusted with white. Hangs from a leaf or stem by the tail and a silk midriff girdle. **VARIATION** Sexually dimorphic. ♀ has variable yellow on upper side hind wings. There are three subspecies, all similar. **SIMILAR SPECIES** ♂ Cambridge Vagrant (p. 116) is pale blue and smaller. ♀ Twin (p. 125) and Common (p. 126) dotted borders are smaller and fly more slowly. **STATUS** Scarce but widespread.

J F M A M J J A S O N D

## Buquet's Vagrant
Buquet-swerwer
*Nepheronia buquetii buquetii*      **45–56 mm**

**HABITS** Fast wandering flight at or above head height. ♀ slower than ♂. Found near food plants. **HABITAT** Coastal bush, savanna and forest. **EARLY STAGES** *Egg* an elongated fluted oval. White to cream. Laid singly on *Azima tetracantha*. *Larva* up to 35 mm. Cylindrical. Deep green with a thin yellow dorsal line. *Pupa* up to 24 mm. Flattened laterally with wing cases forming a semicircular frontal keel. Leaf green. Hangs from a leaf or stem by the tail and a silk midriff girdle. **VARIATION** Sexes similar. **SIMILAR SPECIES** African Migrant (p. 112), but Buquet's is never yellow and its upper side forewing has a dark margin. **STATUS** Scarce but widespread.

J F M A M J J A S O N D

## Cambridge Vagrant
**Blouswerwer**
*Nepheronia thalassina sinalata*      **50–60 mm**

**HABITS** ♂ flight fast and direct, above head height or higher. ♀ is slower and stays near food plants. **HABITAT** Dry and riverine forest. **EARLY STAGES** *Egg* an elongated fluted oval. Yellow. Laid singly on *Hippocratea longipetiolata*, *H. africana* or a *Jasminium*. *Larva* up to 37 mm. Cylindrical. Deep green with a thin yellow dorsal line and white lateral spots on the thoracic segments. *Pupa* up to 29 mm. Flattened laterally. Wing cases form a semicircular frontal keel. Pale green. Hangs from a leaf or stem by the tail and a silk midriff girdle. **VARIATION** Sexually dimorphic, as shown. ♀ has variable yellow on upper side hind wing. **SIMILAR SPECIES** Large Vagrant (p. 115) ♂ is larger and pale green, not blue. ♀ lacks orange basal patches on underside forewing. **STATUS** Locally common.

J F M A M J J A S O N D

## Veined Tip
**Bontarabier**
*Colotis vesta argillaceus*      **32–45 mm**

**HABITS** Low slow flight relative to other *Colotis* butterflies. Fond of flowers. **HABITAT** Mesic to arid savanna. **EARLY STAGES** *Egg* a fluted oval. White, turning yellow. Laid singly on a *Boscia*, *Capparis* or *Maerua* or on *Salvadora persica*. *Larva* up to 23 mm. Cylindrical. Deep green with yellow dorsal line. *Pupa* up to 14 mm. Wing cases form a semicircular frontal keel. Pale green to yellow-brown with variable black markings. Hangs from a leaf or stem by the tail and a silk midriff girdle. **VARIATION** Sexes similar. Wet season form *pluvius* (not shown) has yellow ground colour and more extensive dark markings. **SIMILAR SPECIES** Topaz Arab (N. Cape, NW, Gau., Mpu., KZN) and Desert Veined Tip (N. Cape) both have less extensive black markings and paler ground colour. **STATUS** Common and widespread.

J F M A M J J A S O N D

PIERIDAE: PIERINAE / TIPS

## Lilac Tip
Boomwagter
*Colotis celimene*

32–40 mm

**HABITS** Fast sustained flight. ♂ is territorial and hovers around large isolated trees at a height of about 5 m. **HABITAT** Arid savanna. **EARLY STAGES** *Egg* a fluted oval. White, turning red. Laid singly on a *Boscia*, *Capparis* or *Maerua*. *Larva* up to 20 mm. Cylindrical. Deep green with cream-white dorsal line and faint white lateral lines. *Pupa* up to 15 mm. Wing cases form a semicircular frontal keel. Varies from pale green to cream. Hangs from a leaf or stem by the tail and a silk midriff girdle. **VARIATION** Sexually dimorphic, as shown. ♀ of smaller subspecies *pholoe* (N. Cape) has some purple at tip of upper side forewing. **SIMILAR SPECIES** Large upper side forewing tip makes this butterfly unique. **STATUS** Scarce and local.

J F M A M J J A S O N D

## Bushveld Purple Tip
Bosveld-perspuntjie
*Colotis ione*

45–52 mm

**HABITS** ♂ flight fast, sustained, at 1–2 m. ♀ is slower and frequents bushes. Fond of flowers. **HABITAT** Savanna. **EARLY STAGES** *Egg* a fluted oval. White, turning pink. Laid singly on a *Boscia*, *Capparis* or *Maerua*. *Larva* up to 24 mm. Cylindrical. Deep green with pale dorsal line and a row of cream lateral blotches. *Pupa* up to 22 mm. Wing cases form a frontal keel. Pale green to cream-white. Hangs from a leaf by the tail and a silk midriff girdle. **VARIATION** Sexually dimorphic, as shown. Fewer dark markings in intermediate and dry season forms (♀ images). Many named ♀ forms; most with orange wing tips, rarely black or buff. **SIMILAR SPECIES** ♂ Coast Purple Tip (E. Cape to KZN) has four, not five, purple wing-tip spots. **STATUS** Common and widespread.

J F M A M J J A S O N D

## Queen Purple Tip
Koninginperspuntjie
*Colotis regina*            45–62 mm

**HABITS** ♂ flight fast and sustained, at height of 1–2 m. ♀ is slower and stays near food plants. **HABITAT** Savanna. **EARLY STAGES Egg** details not recorded. Laid on a *Boscia* or *Capparis*. **Larva** up to 35 mm. Cylindrical. Deep green with paler dorsal line and cream lateral stripe. **Pupa** up to 30 mm. Wing cases form a frontal keel. Pale green. Hangs from a leaf or stem by the tail and a silk midriff girdle. **VARIATION** Sexually dimorphic, as shown. Wet season form (inset) has heavy black veins on upper side. **SIMILAR SPECIES** Bushveld Purple Tip (p. 117) is smaller and the ♂ has smaller wing tips, while the ♀ often has orange wing tips. **STATUS** Scarce but widespread.

| J | F | M | A | M | J | J | A | S | O | N | D |

## Scarlet Tip
Skarlakenpuntjie
*Colotis annae annae*        35–55 mm

**HABITS** Slow wandering flight close to the ground. Fond of flowers. Usually stays near food plants. **HABITAT** Savanna. **EARLY STAGES Egg** oval. Whitish-yellow, developing red blotches. Laid singly on a *Cadaba* or on *Maerua angolensis*. **Larva** up to 25 mm. Cylindrical. Green with paler dorsal line. May have one or two cream lateral spots. **Pupa** up to 20 mm. Wing cases form a frontal keel. Pale green. Hangs from a leaf or stem by the tail and a silk midriff girdle. **VARIATION** Sexually dimorphic, as shown. Dry season forms paler. ♀ wing tip colour varies from yellow to red. **SIMILAR SPECIES** ♀ dry season form (not shown) resembles ♀ Sulphur Orange Tip (p. 119). **STATUS** Common and widespread.

| J | F | M | A | M | J | J | A | S | O | N | D |

PIERIDAE: PIERINAE / TIPS

## Sulphur Orange Tip
Swaeloranjepuntjie
*Colotis auxo auxo*      35–40 mm

**HABITS** Quick fluttering flight close to the ground. Fond of flowers. Usually stays close to food plants. **HABITAT** Savanna. **EARLY STAGES** *Egg* oval. Whitish-yellow, developing pink-brown blotches. Laid singly on a *Cadaba*. *Larva* cylindrical. Green with paler dorsal line and may have a cream lateral line and cream spots. *Pupa* size not recorded. Wing cases form a frontal keel. Green to cream or buff with variable black blotches. Hangs from a leaf or stem by the tail and a silk midriff girdle. **VARIATION** Sexually dimorphic, as shown. Dry season forms (♂ and inset) are paler. ♀ has several named forms, which may lack orange wing tips and have yellow or white ground colour. **SIMILAR SPECIES** ♀ may resemble ♀ Scarlet Tip (p. 118). **STATUS** Common and widespread.

J F M A M J J A S O N D

## Red Tip
Rooioranjepuntjie
*Colotis antevippe gavisa*      40–45 mm

**HABITS** Fast low flight. Fond of flowers. Mostly stays close to food plants. **HABITAT** Savanna and coastal bush. **EARLY STAGES** *Egg* oval. Whitish-yellow, developing red blotches. Laid singly on a *Boscia*, *Capparis* or *Maerua*. *Larva* size not recorded. Cylindrical. Green to dark brown with yellow longitudinal stripes. *Pupa* size not recorded. Wing cases form a frontal keel. Lilac to pale green or buff. Hangs from a leaf or stem by the tail and a silk midriff girdle. **VARIATION** Sexually dimorphic, as shown. Dry season form (inset) has sparser dark markings. **SIMILAR SPECIES** Common and Smoky orange tips (p. 120). Common Orange Tip ♂ has bulge in dark basal edge of wing tip, while Smoky has paler orange wing tip. **STATUS** Common and widespread.

J F M A M J J A S O N D

## Common Orange Tip
Oranjepuntjie
*Colotis evenina evenina*      35–45 mm

**HABITS** Fast low flight. Fond of flowers. Usually stays close to food plants. **HABITAT** Savanna. **EARLY STAGES** *Egg* details not fully recorded, but female known to lay singly on a *Boscia* or *Capparis*. *Larva* up to 25 mm. Cylindrical. Dark green with a white lateral stripe. *Pupa* up to 18 mm. Wing cases form a frontal keel. Green with purple flush. Hangs from a leaf or stem by the tail and a silk midriff girdle. **VARIATION** Sexually dimorphic, as shown. Dry season form (not shown) has fewer dark markings. **SIMILAR SPECIES** Red Tip (p. 119) ♂ forewing tip has a patch of red that varies in size and tint, while Smoky Orange Tip (below) has bulge in dark basal edge to forewing tip. **STATUS** Common and widespread.

## Smoky Orange Tip
Donkeroranjepuntjie
*Colotis euippe omphale*      35–45 cm

**HABITS** Fast low flight. Fond of flowers. Usually stays near food plants. **HABITAT** Savanna, thickets and forest. Absent only from very arid karoo vegetation. **EARLY STAGES** *Egg* oval. White, turning yellow with red marks. Laid singly on a *Boscia*, *Cadaba*, *Capparis* or *Maerua*. *Larva* up to 22 mm. Cylindrical. Green with a white lateral stripe. *Pupa* up to 17 mm. Wing cases form a frontal keel. Green to pale brown. Hangs from a leaf or stem by the tail and a silk midriff girdle. **VARIATION** Sexually dimorphic, as shown. Dry season form (inset) has far sparser dark markings. **SIMILAR SPECIES** Other orange tips lack the distinct bulge in the dark basal edge of the orange forewing tip. **STATUS** Common and widespread.

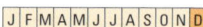

# Small Orange Tip
**Kleinoranjepuntjie**
*Colotis evagore antigone*          **28–38 mm**

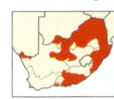

**HABITS** Slow, low, wandering flight. Fond of flowers. **HABITAT** Savanna. Absent from karoo and fynbos. **EARLY STAGES** *Egg* oval. White, turning pink with red marks. Laid singly on a *Cadaba*, *Capparis* or *Maerua*. *Larva* up to 22 mm. Cylindrical. Green with a dark dorsal and a white lateral stripe. *Pupa* up to 17 mm. Wing cases form a frontal keel. Green to pale brown or cream. Hangs from a leaf or stem by the tail and a silk midriff girdle. **VARIATION** Sexually dimorphic, as shown. Fewer dark markings in dry season form (not shown). ♀ may have black or orange forewing tips. **SIMILAR SPECIES** Bushveld (absent only from W. Cape) and Kalahari (N. Cape and NW) orange tips. ♂ told from these orange tips by absence of black marginal spot at base of orange tip, while ♀ lacks orange on underside forewing tip. **STATUS** Common and widespread.

| J | F | M | A | M | J | J | A | S | O | N | D |

# Banded Gold Tip
**Goudpuntjie**
*Teracolus eris eris*          **40–45 mm**

**HABITS** Rapid direct flight at 1–2 m. Fond of flowers. **HABITAT** Savanna. Absent from succulent karoo, fynbos and montane grassland vegetation. **EARLY STAGES** *Egg* oval. White, developing red bands. Laid singly on a *Boscia*. *Larva* up to 27 mm. Cylindrical. Dark green with white dorsal and lateral stripes. *Pupa* up to 20 mm. Wing cases form a shallow keel in front. Green to buff. Hangs from a leaf or stem by the tail and a silk midriff girdle. **VARIATION** Sexually dimorphic, as shown. Dry season form (bottom image) has fewer dark markings and underside hind wing is often pink. ♀ of this form may have brown forewing tips. **SIMILAR SPECIES** ♂ unique owing to jet black basal band in upper side forewing. ♀ similar to Bushveld Purple Tip (p. 117), but smaller and never with orange forewing tip. **STATUS** Common and widespread.

| J | F | M | A | M | J | J | A | S | O | N | D |

## False Dotted Border
Vals-voëlentwitjie
*Belenois thysa thysa* 45–62 mm

**HABITS** Rapid, direct flight along forest edge. ♀ usually seen near food plants. **HABITAT** Coastal and riverine bush. **EARLY STAGES** *Egg* a fluted oval. Pale yellow, turning salmon. Laid singly on a *Boscia*, *Capparis* or *Maerua*. *Larva* up to 37 mm. Cylindrical, tapering towards tail. Back green with yellow, black and white dorsal stripes. *Pupa* up to 26 mm. Green with prominent nose horn and tiny yellow warts. Attached to a leaf or stem by the tail and a silk midriff girdle. **VARIATION** Sexually dimorphic, as shown. Dry season form *vansoni* (not shown) has reduced dark markings. ♀ of this form is orange-buff. **SIMILAR SPECIES** True dotted borders (pp. 125–6) have a single row of spots on hind wing margin. **STATUS** Scarce but widespread.

J F M A M J J A S O N D

## Brown-veined White
Grasveldwitjie
*Belenois aurota* 40–50 mm

**HABITS** Rapid direct flight in one direction. Often seen migrating in large numbers. **HABITAT** Favours arid Kalahari savanna but may be found throughout SA. **EARLY STAGES** *Egg* elongated, conical and ribbed. White, turning pale yellow. Laid in clusters on a *Boscia*, *Capparis* or *Maerua*. *Larva* up to 25 mm. Cylindrical, tapering towards tail. Back green-brown with yellow, black and white dorsal stripes. *Pupa* up to 20 mm. Blunt-headed with short nose horn. Green to pale brown or white with dark marks. Attached to a leaf or stem by the tail and a silk midriff girdle. **VARIATION** Sexually dimorphic, as shown. **SIMILAR SPECIES** African Veined White (throughout SA) larger with more pointed wing tips and has white and yellow ♀ forms, whereas Brown-veined Whites are always white. **STATUS** Common and widespread.

J F M A M J J A S O N D

PIERIDAE: PIERINAE / WHITES

## African Common White
Afrikaanse gewone witjie
*Belenois creona severina*  40–45 mm

**HABITS** Slow wandering flight. Fond of flowers. ♂ frequents mud puddles. **HABITAT** Warm savanna and forest margins. **EARLY STAGES** *Egg* an elongated ribbed cone. White, turning pale yellow. Laid in clusters on a *Boscia*, *Capparis* or *Maerua*. *Larva* up to 25 mm. Cylindrical, tapering towards tail. Back green to yellow or grey-blue with yellow, black and white dorsal stripes. *Pupa* up to 20 mm. Green to brown or cream-white with dark marks and a short nose horn that also bears dark marks. Attached to a leaf or twig by the tail and a silk midriff girdle. **VARIATION** Sexually dimorphic, as shown. **SIMILAR SPECIES** ♂ upper side resembles that of ♀ Lilac Tip (p. 117). **STATUS** Common and widespread.

J F M A M J J A S O N D

## Ant-heap White
Miershoopwitjie
*Dixeia pigea*  40–52 mm

**HABITS** ♂ flies rapidly along forest edge and frequents mud puddles. ♀ is slower and remains in understorey. **HABITAT** Forest and moist woodlands. **EARLY STAGES** *Egg* an elongated ribbed cone. Pale yellow. Laid in a cluster on a *Capparis*. *Larva* up to 30 mm. Cylindrical. Yellow-green with a yellow dorsal stripe and a dual row of yellow dorsal blotches. *Pupa* up to 20 mm. Diamond-shaped with lateral spines at base of abdomen and a short nose horn. Green to yellow. Attached to a leaf or twig by the tail and a silk midriff girdle. **VARIATION** Sexually dimorphic, as shown. ♀ forms *luteola* and *rubrobasalis* (not shown) are cream to yellow-orange. **SIMILAR SPECIES** African Small (Mpu., Swa., KZN and E. Cape) and Black-veined (KZN, Mpu., Lim.) whites lack ochre costal edge to underside hind wing. **STATUS** Common and widespread.

J F M A M J J A S O N D

## Diverse Albatross White
**Willawitjie**
*Appias epaphia contracta*      40–50 mm

**HABITS** Fast flight at forest edge, but ♀ is slower, remaining in understorey. ♂ frequents mud puddles. **HABITAT** Forest and moist woodlands. **EARLY STAGES** *Egg* an elongated ribbed cone. White, turning amber yellow. Laid singly on a *Boscia, Cadaba, Capparis, Cleome* or *Maerua*. *Larva* up to 30 mm. Cylindrical. Dark green with yellow dorsal stripe. *Pupa* up to 22 mm. Diamond-shaped with lateral spines at base of abdomen. Nose horn upturned. Light green with brown marks. Attached to a leaf or twig by the tail and a silk midriff girdle. **VARIATION** Sexually dimorphic, as shown. ♀ dry season form *albida* (not shown) has sparser black markings. **SIMILAR SPECIES** ♂ Sabine Albatross White (Lim., Mpu., KZN, E. Cape) lacks yellow basal flush on forewing underside. **STATUS** Scarce but widespread.

| J | F | M | A | M | J | J | A | S | O | N | D |

## Common Meadow White
**Bontrokkie**
*Pontia helice helice*      35–43 cm

**HABITS** Low, slow, fluttering flight. Fond of flowers. ♂ defends hill-top territory. **HABITAT** Grassy areas throughout SA, but absent from forest and very arid karoo and savanna vegetation. **EARLY STAGES** *Egg* an elongated ribbed cone. Pale yellow becoming light orange. Laid singly on one of many different Brassicaceae or Resedaceae. *Larva* up to 28 mm. Cylindrical. Green-grey with a yellow lateral stripe. Covered in small black spots. *Pupa* up to 20 mm. Elongated with short head horn. Light green-grey with yellow stripes. Attached to a leaf or twig by the tail and a silk midriff girdle. **VARIATION** Sexually dimorphic, as shown. **SIMILAR SPECIES** Brown-veined White (p. 122) lacks yellow-green underside hind wing markings. **STATUS** Common and widespread.

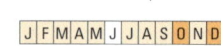

| J | F | M | A | M | J | J | A | S | O | N | D |

## African Wood White
**Fladderpapiertjie**
*Leptosia alcesta inalcesta*   30–42 mm

**HABITS** Halting, weak, slow, low, bouncing flight. Settles often, but restless. **HABITAT** Forest understorey. **EARLY STAGES Egg** ribbed and very elongated. White. Laid singly on a *Capparis* or on *Maerua juncea*. **Larva** up to 22 mm. Cylindrical. Green with faint white lateral stripe. **Pupa** up to 16 mm. Wing cases form a shallow frontal keel. Green. Hangs from a leaf or twig by tail and silk midriff girdle. **VARIATION** Sexes similar. **SIMILAR SPECIES** Large Glasswing (northern KZN) occurs in similar habitat, but flight is faster and fluttering. It also has heavy black forewing borders and a discal band, rather than a spot on upper side forewing. **STATUS** Locally common.

J F M A M J J A S O N D

## Twin Dotted Border
**Oranjevlerk voëlent-witjie**
*Mylothris rueppellii haemus*   48–56 mm

**HABITS** Slow, floating, sailing flight high in tree canopy. Fond of flowers. **HABITAT** Wooded savanna and forest. **EARLY STAGES Egg** barrel-shaped and ribbed. White, coated with a yellow liquid. Laid in clusters on *Ximenia caffra* or any of a range of Loranthaceae. **Larva** up to 30 mm. Cylindrical and covered in short hairs. Dark green with white warts. **Pupa** up to 18 mm. Ornate with upturned nose horn. Varies from white to green, always with yellow and black marks. Attached to a leaf or twig by tail and a silk midriff girdle. **VARIATION** Sexually dimorphic, as shown. **SIMILAR SPECIES** Common Dotted Border (p. 126) lacks orange basal flush in upper side forewing. Trimen's Dotted Border (Lim., Mpu., KZN, E. Cape) has yellow hind wing. **STATUS** Scarce but widespread.

J F M A M J J A S O N D

## Common Dotted Border

Gewone voëlent-witjie
*Mylothris agathina agathina*      50–65 mm

**HABITS** Slow sailing flight in tree tops. Fond of flowers. **HABITAT** Fynbos, savanna and forest. **EARLY STAGES Egg** a ribbed barrel. White, coated with a yellow liquid. Laid in clusters of 45–70 on one of the Loranthaceae or Santalaceae, mostly *Agelanthus* or *Osyris* in SA. **Larva** up to 32 mm. Cylindrical and covered in short hairs. Chocolate with white warts. Gregarious. **Pupa** up to 22 mm. Ornate with upturned nose horn. Cream with black markings. Attached to a leaf or twig by the tail and a silk midriff girdle. **VARIATION** Sexually dimorphic. **SIMILAR SPECIES** Twin Dotted Border (p. 125) has orange basal flush on upper side forewing. Trimen's Dotted Border (Lim., Mpu., KZN, E. Cape) has yellow hind wing. **STATUS** Common and widespread.

| J | F | M | A | M | J | J | A | S | O | N | D |

## Bush Kite Swallowtail

Vlieëndepiering-swaelstert
*Papilio euphranor*      80–110 mm

**HABITS** ♂ soars in the forest canopy. ♀ flies along forest edges. Both sexes fond of red flowers. **HABITAT** Afrotemperate and, occasionally, coastal forest. **EARLY STAGES Egg** spherical with no texture, like all swallow- and swordtail eggs. Pale yellow-green, developing red-brown spots. Laid singly on a leaf of *Cryptocarya woodii*. **Larva** up to 42 mm. Thicker at thorax. Leaf green with black spots, white transverse bands and four concentric double black rings across the thorax. **Pupa** up to 28 mm. Leaf-like with short head horns. Green. Attached to a leaf or twig by the tail and a silk midriff girdle. **VARIATION** Sexes similar. ♀ has double discal band on upper side forewing. **SIMILAR SPECIES** Constantine's Swallowtail (p. 128) has yellow spot in forewing cell. **STATUS** Scarce but local.

| J | F | M | A | M | J | J | A | S | O | N | D |

**PAPILIONIDAE: PAPILIONINAE / SWALLOWTAILS** 127

# Mocker Swallowtail (♀)
# Flying Handkerchief (♂)
**Na-aper swaelstert**

*Papilio dardanus cenea*   80–110 mm

**HABITS** ♂ conspicuous in flight, leisurely but erratic. ♀ flight low and slow, near food plants. **HABITAT** Afrotemperate and coastal forest. **EARLY STAGES** *Egg* spherical. White, developing ring of brown spots. Laid singly on Rutaceae. *Larva* up to 35 mm. Thickened at thorax. Green with lacy white markings and rows of sky blue spots. Small black thoracic eyespots. *Pupa* up to 35 mm. Leaf-like. Yellow-green dorsally, dull green ventrally with yellow lateral line. Attached to a leaf or twig by the tail and a silk midriff girdle. **VARIATION** Sexually dimorphic, as shown. Several ♀ forms, including those shown here. **SIMILAR SPECIES** ♂ unique. ♀ mimics African Monarch (p. 20), Friar (p.20), Layman (p. 21) and others. **STATUS** Common and widespread.

J F M A M J J A S O N D

trophonius
cenea

hippocoonides

# White-banded Swallowtail
**Witlint-swaelstert**
*Papilio echerioides echerioides*   65–75 mm

**HABITS** Low, slow, fluttering flight. Often visits flowers. ♂ frequents mud puddles. **HABITAT** Afrotemperate and coastal forest. **EARLY STAGES** *Egg* spherical. Pale yellow, developing red-brown spots. Laid singly on leaf of a Rutaceae, especially *Clausena anisata*, or on a *Citrus*. *Larva* up to 32 mm. Thickened at thorax. Bright moss green with irregular pale brown bands and small black thoracic eyespots. *Pupa* up to 30 mm. Wing cases protrude. Head ornate. Green. White and yellow markings on thorax and abdominal processes. Attached to a leaf or twig by the tail and a silk midriff girdle. **VARIATION** Sexually dimorphic, as shown. **SIMILAR SPECIES** ♂ resembles White-barred Charaxes (p. 49), but underside and habits distinctive. ♀ mimics Layman (p. 21). **STATUS** Locally common.

J F M A M J J A S O N D

## Constantine's Swallowtail
Konstantyn-se-swaelstert
*Papilio constantinus constantinus*     **70–95 mm**

**HABITS** Low, slow, fluttering flight. Visits flowers often. ♂ frequents mud puddles. **HABITAT** Forest and wooded savanna. **EARLY STAGES** *Egg* spherical. Pale yellow, developing a ring of brown spots. Laid singly on a leaf of one of the Rutaceae, such as a *Citrus*. Often also on *Vepris reflexa*. *Larva* up to 33 mm. Thickened at thorax. Green with fine white speckling, a double row of sky blue spots and small black thoracic eyespots. *Pupa* up to 33 mm. Leaf-like with short head horns. Green. Attached to a leaf or twig by the tail and a silk midriff girdle. **VARIATION** Sexes similar. **SIMILAR SPECIES** Bush Kite Swallowtail (p. 126) lacks yellow spot in forewing cell. **STATUS** Scarce but widespread.

J F M A M J J A S O N D

## Citrus Swallowtail
Lemoenskoenlapper
*Papilio demodocus demodocus*     **90–110 mm**

**HABITS** Fast direct flight. Fond of flowers. ♂ frequents mud puddles and defends hill-top territory. **HABITAT** All vegetation types other than very arid Nama karoo. **EARLY STAGES** *Egg* spherical. Pale yellow, developing light brown spots. Laid singly on a leaf of one of the Rutaceae or Apiaciae, especially a *Citrus* or *Peucedanum*. *Larva* up to 40 mm. Thickened at thorax. Form found on Rutaceae is green with irregular white or grey bands. Form on Apiaceae is cream with black stripes and yellow spots. *Pupa* up to 36 mm. Resembles broken twig. Yellow dorsally, green ventrally with green or brown abdomen. Attached to a leaf or twig by the tail and a silk midriff girdle. **VARIATION** Sexes similar. **SIMILAR SPECIES** Constantine's (above), Bush Kite (p. 126) and Emperor (p. 129) swallowtails all have tails. **STATUS** Common and widespread.

J F M A M J J A S O N D

## Green-banded Swallowtail
**Groenlint-swaelstert**
*Papilio nireus lyaeus*     **75–95 mm**

**HABITS** Fast direct flight. Fond of flowers. ♂ frequents mud puddles. **HABITAT** Forest, savanna and gardens. **EARLY STAGES** *Egg* spherical. Pale cream, developing red-brown spots. Laid singly on a leaf of one of the Rutaceae or Apiaciae, especially a *Citrus* or *Peucedanum*. **Larva** up to 32 mm. Thickened at thorax. Bright green with fine white speckling, yellow lateral stripes and black thoracic eyespots. *Pupa* up to 30 mm. Leaf-like with a pair of blunt head processes. Green or brown. Attached to a leaf or twig by the tail and a silk midriff girdle. **VARIATION** Sexes similar, but ♀ has greenish bands. **SIMILAR SPECIES** Unique in SA. **STATUS** Common and widespread.

J F M A M J J A S O N D

## Emperor Swallowtail
**Koning-swaelstert**
*Papilio ophidicephalus*     **100–135 mm**

**HABITS** Fast undulating flight along streams and gullies. ♂ frequents mud puddles. **HABITAT** Afrotemperate and coastal forest. **EARLY STAGES** *Egg* spherical. Pale yellow, turning a darker, dull yellow. Laid singly on leaf of a *Calodendron*, *Clausena* or *Zanthoxylon*. **Larva** up to 45 mm. Thickened at thorax. Bright green with fine speckling, yellow lateral stripes and black thoracic eyespots. *Pupa* up to 40 mm. Mottled green, black and brown to resemble broken twig covered in lichen. Attached to a leaf or twig by the tail and a silk midriff girdle. **VARIATION** Sexes similar. Five geographic subspecies (including *phalusco* shown here) all with slight differences in upper side forewing discal bands. **SIMILAR SPECIES** Bush Kite (p. 126) and Constantine's (p. 128) swallowtails are smaller and lack blue marks on upper side hind wing. **STATUS** Local and fairly uncommon.

J F M A M J J A S O N D

## White Lady
Witnooientjie
*Graphium morania*      50–60 mm

**HABITS** Fast erratic flight at or above head height. ♂ frequents mud puddles. **HABITAT** Warm savanna and coastal bush. **EARLY STAGES** *Egg* spherical. Pale green-yellow. Laid singly on a leaf of *Annona senegalensis, Artrabotrys, Hexalobus monopetalus* or *Uvaria caffra*. *Larva* up to 30 mm. Tapers towards tail. Bright green with three pairs of short black thoracic spines. *Pupa* 25 mm. Leaf-like with large dorsal projection on thorax. Green, buff or brown. Attached to a leaf or twig by the tail and a silk midriff girdle. **VARIATION** Sexes similar. **SIMILAR SPECIES** Angola White-lady Swordtail (KZN to Gau., Lim.) has black line through white blotch at outer end of forewing cell. **STATUS** Locally common.

| J | F | M | A | M | J | J | A | S | O | N | D |

## Veined Swordtail
Bont-swaardstert
*Graphium leonidas leonidas*      75–85 mm

**HABITS** Fast erratic flight at or above head height. ♂ frequents mud puddles and defends hill-top territory. **HABITAT** Warm savanna and coastal bush. **EARLY STAGES** *Egg* spherical. Pale yellow. Laid singly on a shoot of an Annonaceae, such as *Annona senegalensis, Monanthotaxis caffra* or *Uvaria caffra*. *Larva* up to 45 mm. Tapers towards tail. Green ventrally, pale blue-green dorsally. Three pairs of short black thoracic spines and a deep green to brown dorsal patch on thorax. *Pupa* up to 33 mm. Leaf-like with large dorsal projection on thorax. Green. Attached to a leaf or twig by the tail and a silk midriff girdle. **VARIATION** Sexes similar. **SIMILAR SPECIES** Like ♂ Forest Queen (p. 54), mimics the rare vagrant Blue (Dappled) Monarch (Lim.). **STATUS** Common and widespread.

| J | F | M | A | M | J | J | A | S | O | N | D |

## Large Striped Swordtail
Jag-swaardstert
*Graphium antheus*          **65–75 mm**

**HABITS** Fast erratic flight, at or above head height. ♂ frequents mud puddles. **HABITAT** Warm savanna and coastal bush. **EARLY STAGES** *Egg* spherical. Pale green. Laid singly on a shoot of an Annonaceae like *Annona senegalensis*, *Monanthotaxis caffra* or *Hexalobus monopetalus*. *Larva* up to 35 mm. Tapers towards tail. Two forms, both with three pairs of short thoracic spines. One form is green with dark spines, the other chocolate with yellow spines and a yellow thoracic band. *Pupa* up to 23 mm. Leaf-like with large dorsal projection on thorax. Green or pale brown. Attached to a leaf or twig by the tail and a silk midriff girdle. **VARIATION** Sexes similar. **SIMILAR SPECIES** Small Striped Swordtail (below) has straight bars in forewing cell. **STATUS** Common and widespread.

## Small Striped Swordtail
Ooskus-swaardstert
*Graphium policenes policenes*      **55–65 mm**

**HABITS** Fast erratic flight at or above head height. ♂ frequents mud puddles. **HABITAT** Coastal bush. **EARLY STAGES** *Egg* spherical. Pale green-yellow. Laid singly on a shoot of an Annonaceae like *Annona senegalensis*, *Monanthotaxis caffra* or *Uvaria caffra*. *Larva* up to 32 mm. Tapers towards tail. Three pairs of short black thoracic spines and a black thoracic band. Two forms, one yellow with cream and brown transverse bands, the other leaf green with broad, darker green dorsal bands. *Pupa* 24 mm. Leaf-like with large dorsal projection on thorax. Green. Attached to a leaf or twig by the tail and a silk midriff girdle. **VARIATION** Sexes similar. **SIMILAR SPECIES** Large Striped Swordtail (above) has wavy bars in forewing cell. **STATUS** Locally common.

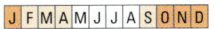

## Cream-striped Swordtail
**Kwagga-swaardstert**
*Graphium porthaon porthaon*          55–65 mm

**HABITS** Fast erratic flight at or above head height. ♂ frequents mud puddles. **HABITAT** Coastal bush and warm savanna. **EARLY STAGES** *Egg* spherical. Whitish-yellow. Laid singly on shoot of an Annonaceae like *Monodora junodii, Monanthotaxis caffra* or *Uvaria caffra*. *Larva* up to 32 mm. Tapers towards tail. Two forms occur, one yellow to green with yellow lateral stripes, the other with alternating black, yellow and white bands. Both forms have three pairs of short black thoracic spines. *Pupa* up to 24 mm. Leaf-like with large dorsal projection on thorax. Green to pale brown. Attached to a leaf or twig by the tail and a silk midriff girdle. **VARIATION** Sexes similar. **SIMILAR SPECIES** Large Striped Swordtail (p. 131) has turquoise markings. Mamba Swordtail (KZN) is darker with green stripes. **STATUS** Locally common.

J F M A M J J A S O N D

## Striped Policeman
**Witbroek-konstabel**
*Coeliades forestan forestan*          42–64 mm

**HABITS** Powerful irregular flight at or above head height. ♂ scent-marks his territory. **HABITAT** Coastal bush, forest and warm savanna. **EARLY STAGES** *Egg* a ribbed dome. White, turning pink. Laid singly on a shoot of one of many plants in the Fabaceae, Combretaceae or Malpighiaceae. *Larva* up to 40 mm. Cylindrical with neck-like narrowing behind head. White with maroon and yellow bands. Head yellow with black spots. Shelter comprises leaves folded and stitched with silk. *Pupa* up to 23 mm. Oval. Green, covered in white powder. Forms in larval shelter. **VARIATION** Sexes similar. **SIMILAR SPECIES** Two-pip (p. 133) and One-pip (Lim., Mpu., KZN) policemen have black spots in white patch on upper side hind wing. **STATUS** Common and widespread.

J F M A M J J A S O N D

HESPERIIDAE: COELIADINAE / POLICEMEN   133

# Two-pip Policeman
Dubbelkol-konstabel
*Coeliades pisistratus*   55–70 mm

**HABITS** Fast erratic flight at or above head height. ♂ territorial. Both sexes found on flowers. **HABITAT** Coastal bush and savanna. **EARLY STAGES** *Egg* domed and ribbed. White, turning pink. Laid singly on a shoot of one of the Fabaceae, Combretaceae or Malpighiaceae, often a *Sphedamnocarpus* or *Acridocarpus*. *Larva* up to 45 mm. Cylindrical with neck-like narrowing behind head. White with black and yellow bands. Head yellow with black spots. Shelter comprises leaves folded and stitched with silk. *Pupa* up to 24 mm. Oval. Green, covered in white powder. Forms in larval shelter. **VARIATION** Sexes similar. **SIMILAR SPECIES** One-pip Policeman (Lim., Mpu., KZN) has single spot in white patch on upper side hind wing. **STATUS** Common and widespread.

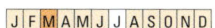

# Red-tab Policeman
Rooibroek-konstabel
*Coeliades keithloa*   58–66 mm

**HABITS** Skipping, hopping flight along forest edges. ♂ territorial. Both sexes found on flowers. **HABITAT** Coastal bush and forest. **EARLY STAGES** *Egg* a ribbed dome. Cream, turning pink. Laid singly on a leaf or stem of *Acridocarpus natalitius* or *Barringtonia racemosa*. *Larva* up to 45 mm. Cylindrical with neck-like narrowing behind head. White with maroon and yellow bands. Head yellow with black spots. Shelter comprises leaves folded and stitched shut with silk. *Pupa* up to 24 mm. Oval. Green, covered in white powder. Forms in larval shelter. **VARIATION** Sexes similar. **SIMILAR SPECIES** Lorenzo or Coastal Red-tab policemen (Lim., northern KZN) almost identical and separated from Red-table Policeman only by dissection, although the larvae differ. **STATUS** Locally common.

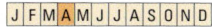

### Christmas Forester
Kersfees-bosjagtertjie
*Celaenorrhinus mokeezi*     40–51 mm

**HABITS** Rapid, low, skipping flight in forest glades and clearings. ♂ territorial. **HABITAT** Coastal and montane forest. **EARLY STAGES** *Egg* a ribbed dome. White, developing red apical spot. Laid singly on a leaf of *Isoglossa woodii*. *Larva* up to 28 mm. Cylindrical with neck-like narrowing behind head. Green with a dark dorsal stripe. Head pale brown. Shelter comprises leaves folded and stitched with silk. *Pupa* up to 23 mm. Oval with blunt head. Tapers towards tail. Green, covered in white powder. Forms in larval shelter. **VARIATION** Sexes similar. Subspecies *separata* (north of Tugela River) has more prominent marginal spots on upper side hind wing than nominate (Knysna to Tugela River). **SIMILAR SPECIES** Unique in SA. **STATUS** Locally common.

J F M A M J J A S O N D

### Clouded Forester
Skaduwee-dartelaartjie
*Tagiades flesus*     35–49 mm

**HABITS** Rapid dancing flight in shady forest clearings, where white of underside hind wing is conspicuous. ♂ territorial. **HABITAT** Coastal forest and woodlands. **EARLY STAGES** *Egg* a ribbed dome covered in anal scales transferred from the ♀. White, turning red. Laid singly on leaf of a *Dioscoria*. *Larva* up to 28 mm. Cylindrical with neck-like narrowing behind head. Shiny purple to green. Head red-brown. Shelter comprises leaves folded and stitched with silk. *Pupa* up to 20 mm. Oval with blunt head. Tapers towards tail. Brown and white, covered in white powder. Forms in larval shelter. **VARIATION** Sexes similar. **SIMILAR SPECIES** Rufous-winged Elfin (eastern W. Cape to Lim.) has larger hyaline spots on forewing. One form lacks white on underside hind wing. **STATUS** Common and widespread.

J F M A M J J A S O N D

## Marbled Elf
Marmer-kluisenaar
*Eretis djaelaelae*          **31–46 mm**

**HABITS** Fast, low, skipping flight. Settles on the ground or low vegetation with wings wide open. ♂ territorial. **HABITAT** Woodlands and savanna. **EARLY STAGES Egg** a ribbed dome. Yellow, turning red. Laid singly on a leaf of *Asystasia gangetica*, *Chaetacanthus setiger* or *Phaulopsis imbricata* or else a *Dyschoriste* or *Justicia*. **Larva** up to 17 mm. Cylindrical and hairy with neck-like narrowing behind head. Grey-brown. Shelter comprises leaves folded and stitched with silk. **Pupa** up to 17 mm. Oval, tapering to the tail. Head blunt. Grey-white. Forms in larval shelter. **VARIATION** Sexes similar. **SIMILAR SPECIES** Small Marbled Elf (eastern SA, south coast to W. Cape) has brown, not white, forelegs. **STATUS** Widespread but scarce.

J F M A M J J A S O N D

## Elfin Skipper
Motozi-kaboutertjie
*Sarangesa motozi*          **36–40 mm**

**HABITS** Fast, low, skipping flight in shade. Settles on the ground or low plants, wings wide open. Roosts in animal burrows. **HABITAT** Woodlands and forest. **EARLY STAGES Egg** a ribbed dome. White, turning red. Laid singly on leaf of *Diclyptera hensii* or a *Barleria* or *Justicia*. **Larva** up to 21 mm. Cylindrical with neck-like narrowing behind head, as is typical of a skipper. Green with darker dorsal stripe and brown head. Shelter comprises leaves folded and stitched together with silk. **Pupa** up to 17 mm. Oval with blunt head. Pale green. Forms in larval shelter. **VARIATION** Sexes similar. Winter form *pertusa* has less mottling and more geometric upper side patterning. **SIMILAR SPECIES** Ruona, Small and Dark elfins (eastern and northern SA) lack the hyaline spots on hind wing. **STATUS** Common and widespread.

J F M A M J J A S O N D

## Buff-tipped Skipper
Bruinpunt-dartelaartjie
*Netrobalane canopus*      26–45 mm

**HABITS** Fast skipping flight on forest edge. Settles with wings wide open. ♂ defends hill-top territory. **HABITAT** Warm savanna and forest. **EARLY STAGES** *Egg* a ribbed dome covered in anal scales transferred from ♀. Pale yellow, turning salmon pink. Laid singly on a leaf of a *Dombeya*, *Grewia*, *Hibiscus* or *Pavonia*. *Larva* up to 26 mm. Cylindrical with neck-like narrowing behind head, as is typical for a skipper. Green, covered with short white hairs. Head black. Shelter comprises leaves stitched with silk. *Pupa* up to 21 mm. Oval. Head has short horn. White with black spots. Forms in larval shelter. **VARIATION** Sexes similar. **SIMILAR SPECIES** Only grey-brown Ragged Skipper (NW, Gau., Lim., Mpu., KZN and Swa.) bears any resemblance. **STATUS** Scarce and local.

| J | F | M | A | M | J | J | A | S | O | N | D |

## White-cloaked Skipper
Witjas-dartelaartjie
*Leucochitonea levubu*      30–45 mm

**HABITS** Deceptively fast, skipping flight. ♂ territorial, usually seen on hill-tops. ♀ shy and seldom seen. Both sexes fond of flowers. Occasionally swarms in large numbers. **HABITAT** Dry savanna. **EARLY STAGES** Details not recorded, but ♀ has been observed laying eggs on *Grewia flava*. **VARIATION** Sexes similar. **SIMILAR SPECIES** Unique. **STATUS** Widespread but scarce.

| J | F | M | A | M | J | J | A | S | O | N | D |

## Paradise Skipper
Paradys-dartelaartjie
*Abantis paradisea*      **40–50 mm**

**HABITS** Fast skipping flight on forest edge. Settles with open wings. ♂ defends hill-top territory. **HABITAT** Warm savanna and coastal bush. **EARLY STAGES** *Egg* a ribbed dome covered in anal scales transferred from ♀. Pale yellow. Laid singly on the leaf of a food plant in any of several families, often a *Bridelia* or *Hibiscus*. *Larva* up to 31 mm. Cylindrical with neck-like narrowing behind head. Pale grey with lateral rows of black-centred yellow spots. Head brown. Shelter comprises leaves stitched together with silk. *Pupa* up to 21 mm. Oval with short forked horn on head. White. Forms in larval shelter. **VARIATION** Sexes similar. **SIMILAR SPECIES** Spotted Velvet Skipper (Lim., Mpu., KZN and Swa.) has black spots in white patch on upper side hind wing. **STATUS** Widespread but scarce.

J F M A M J J A S O N D

## Veined Skipper
Vos-dartelaartjie
*Abantis venosa*      **36–45 mm**

**HABITS** Fast skipping flight. Settles with open wings. ♂ territorial, usually found on hill-tops. **HABITAT** Warm savanna. **EARLY STAGES** *Egg* details not fully recorded, but female known to lay eggs on a *Pterocarpus*. *Larva* size not recorded. Cylindrical with neck-like narrowing behind head. Off-white with lateral rows of black-centred yellow spots. Head black with white hairs. Shelter comprises leaves stitched shut with silk. *Pupa* details not recorded. **VARIATION** Sexes similar. Dry season form *umvulensis* lighter in colour than nominate (not shown). **SIMILAR SPECIES** Bi-coloured Skipper (KZN, E. Cape coast) has black blotches on upper side forewing. **STATUS** Widespread but scarce.

J F M A M J J A S O N D

### Forest Sandman
Bos-sandmannetjie
*Spialia dromus*             23–32 mm

**HABITS** Low skipping flight with buzzing wings. Settles with wings three-quarters open. ♂ territorial. **HABITAT** Warm savanna, coastal bush and forest. **EARLY STAGES** *Egg* a ribbed dome. White-green. Laid singly on a shoot of *Triumfetta*, *Melhania* or *Waltheria*. *Larva* up to 20 mm. Cylindrical with neck-like narrowing behind head. Olive green with hairy black head. Shelter comprises leaves stitched together with silk. *Pupa* up to 13 mm. Oval with blunt head. Brown, covered in white powder. Forms in larval shelter. **VARIATION** Sexes similar. **SIMILAR SPECIES** 13 *Spialia* sandmen occur in SA. Told from Mountain Sandman (p. 139) by lack of basal spot on costa and from other sandmen by larger and better-defined spots. **STATUS** Common and widespread.

| J | F | M | A | M | J | J | A | S | O | N | D |

### Common Sandman
Gewone-sandmannetjie
*Spialia diomus ferax*        27–33 mm

**HABITS** Low skipping flight with buzzing wings. Settles with wings three-quarters open. ♂ territorial. **HABITAT** All habitats other than very wet forest and the most arid Nama karoo. **EARLY STAGES** *Egg* a ribbed dome. Pale blue-green. Laid singly on a shoot of *Hermannia*, *Triumfetta*, *Hibiscus*, *Pavonia*, *Sida* or *Waltheria*. *Larva* up to 22 mm. Cylindrical with neck-like narrowing behind head. Greyish-green. Head black and hairy. Shelter comprises leaves stitched with silk. *Pupa* up to 13 mm. Oval with blunt head. Brown, covered in white powder. Forms in larval shelter. **VARIATION** Sexes similar. **SIMILAR SPECIES** 13 similar *Spialia* sandmen occur in SA. Wandering Sandman (NW, Gau., Lim., Mpu., KZN and Swa.) has similar underside hind wing, but upper side forewing lacks basal spots in cell. **STATUS** Common and widespread.

| J | F | M | A | M | J | J | A | S | O | N | D |

HESPERIIDAE: PYRGINAE / SANDMEN, SKIPPERS

# Mountain Sandman
**Berg-sandmannetjie**
*Spialia spio* 22–31 mm

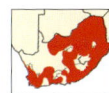

**HABITS** Low, skipping flight with buzzing wings. Settles with wings three-quarters open. ♂ territorial. **HABITAT** Most habitats other than true desert and very arid Nama karoo vegetation. **EARLY STAGES** *Egg* a ribbed dome. Pale green. Laid singly on a shoot of *Hermannia*, *Triumfetta*, *Hibiscus*, *Pavonia*, *Sida* or *Triumfetta*. *Larva* up to 21 mm. Cylindrical with neck-like narrowing behind head. Pale green. Head black and hairy. Shelter comprises leaves stitched shut with silk. *Pupa* up to 12 mm. Oval with blunt head. Green-grey, covered in white powder. Forms in larval shelter. **VARIATION** Sexes similar. **SIMILAR SPECIES** 13 *Spialia* sandmen occur in SA. Mafa Sandman (absent only from arid central regions) has similar underside hind wing but lacks white basal spot on costa in upper side forewing. **STATUS** Common and widespread.

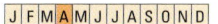

# Green-marbled Skipper
**Asjas-springertjie**
*Gomalia elma* 26–36 mm

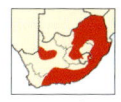

**HABITS** Colonial. Low, skipping flight. Settles frequently with wings held flat. Found near food plants. **HABITAT** Open country in savanna, dry grassland, Nama karoo and forest clearings. **EARLY STAGES** *Egg* a ribbed dome. Pale yellow-brown. Laid singly on a shoot of an *Abutilon* or *Sida*. *Larva* up to 22 mm. Cylindrical with neck-like narrowing behind head. Pale green. Head black and hairy. Shelter comprises leaves stitched with silk. *Pupa* up to 10 mm. Oval with blunt head. Grey-white, covered in white powder. Forms in larval shelter. **VARIATION** Sexes similar. **SIMILAR SPECIES** Unique markings, but resembles a sandman in flight. **STATUS** Widespread but scarce.

## Karoo Dancer
**Karoo-dansertjie**
*Alenia sandaster*  22–28 mm

**HABITS** Colonial. Low, fast, buzzing flight. Often settles on the ground with wings three-quarters open. Found near food plants. **HABITAT** Nama karoo. **EARLY STAGES** *Egg* a ribbed dome. Yellow, turning green then gold. Laid singly on a shoot of *Blepharis capensis* or a *Barleria*. *Larva* up to 17 mm. Cylindrical with neck-like narrowing behind head. Body grey-brown with pale dorsolateral stripes. Head black with yellow hairs. Shelter comprises leaves stitched shut with silk. *Pupa* up to 11 mm. Oval with blunt head. Brown-black, covered in white powder. Forms in larval shelter. **VARIATION** Sexes similar. **SIMILAR SPECIES** Namaqua Dancer (N. Cape) has more extensive white speckling on underside hind wing. **STATUS** Locally common.

## Gold-spotted Sylph
**Reënbos-walsertjie**
*Metisella metis*  26–33 mm

**HABITS** Low fluttering flight in shade. Settles often with wings half open. **HABITAT** Afrotemperate forest. **EARLY STAGES** *Egg* a ribbed hemisphere. White, developing red blotches. Laid singly on *Panicum deustum*, *Setaria megaphylla* or *Stipa dregeana*. *Larva* up to 35 mm. Cylindrical with neck-like narrowing behind head. Grey-green with dark and pale stripes. Constructs shelter of leaves stitched with silk. *Pupa* up to 18 mm. Elongated with pointed ends. Green. Forms in larval shelter. **VARIATION** Sexes similar. Nominate *metis* (west of Swellendam) has larger gold spots than subspecies *paris* (rest of range). **SIMILAR SPECIES** Of the five *Metisella* sylphs, only the Grassveld (Lim. to Les.) and Bamboo (KZN, E. Cape) sylphs are similar with less well-defined markings, and the latter has cream, not gold, spots. **STATUS** Common and widespread.

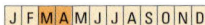

HESPERIIDAE: HETEROPTERINAE / SYLPHS, HESPERIINAE / RANGERS

## Dismal Sylph
Donker-walsertjie
*Tsitana tsita*

**30–38 mm**

**HABITS** Colonial. Low fluttering flight above grass. Often settles on grass or the ground. Fond of flowers. **HABITAT** Grassland. **EARLY STAGES** Nothing recorded, but ♀ observed laying on *Stipa dregeana* grass. **VARIATION** Sexes similar. **SIMILAR SPECIES** Dickson's, Tulbagh (W. Cape and eastern E. Cape) and Uitenhage (eastern W. Cape to E. Cape) sylphs have diagonal cream line on underside hind wing. Modest Sylph (E. Cape to KZN, Les.) has spots on underside hind wing. **STATUS** Common and widespread.

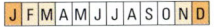

## Barber's Ranger
Barber-se-wagtertjie
*Kedestes barberae*

**26–38 mm**

**HABITS** Fast, low, skipping flight. Settles on grass. Fond of flowers. **HABITAT** Grassland and grassy areas in the Karoo. Also occurs in fynbos. **EARLY STAGES** *Egg* a ribbed dome. White, turning brown. Laid singly on a blade of *Imperata cylindrica* grass. *Larva* up to 27 mm. Cylindrical. Body green. Head pale brown with darker brown marks. Shelter comprises a tube of grass blades stitched with silk. *Pupa* up to 17 mm. Elongated with blunt head and pointed tail. Brown-grey. Forms in larval shelter. **VARIATION** Sexes similar. Two smaller subspecies, *bonsa* (E. Cape mountains) (not shown) and *bunta* (Cape Flats; threatened). **SIMILAR SPECIES** Sarah's Ranger is larger with plainer underside hind wing. **STATUS** Widespread but scarce.

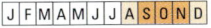

## Wallengren's Ranger
**Wallengren-se-wagtertjie**
*Kedestes wallengrenii*     **27–35 mm**

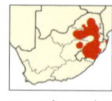

**HABITS** Fast, low, skipping flight. Settles on grass. Fond of flowers. **HABITAT** Long grass near streams and marshes, but sometimes occurs in short grass. **EARLY STAGES** Details not recorded, but ♀ observed laying on the grass *Imperata cylindrica*. **VARIATION** Sexes similar. **SIMILAR SPECIES** Dark (KZN, E. and W. Cape) and Unique (KZN, Les., FS, E. and W. Cape) rangers have silver-white streak along inner margin (not discal area) of underside hind wing. **STATUS** Locally common.

## Macomo Ranger
**Macomo-wagtertjie**
*Kedestes macomo*     **28–35 mm**

**HABITS** Fast, low, skipping flight. Settles on shaded grass. **HABITAT** Grassy areas in wooded savanna and coastal bush. **EARLY STAGES** *Egg* a ribbed dome. White, turning brown. Laid singly on a blade of *Imperata cylindrica*. *Larva* up to 30 mm. Cylindrical. Body greenish-white. Head pale brown with darker brown markings. Constructs a tubular shelter of grass blades and silk. *Pupa* up to 18 mm. Elongated with blunt head and pointed tail. Brown-grey. Forms in larval shelter. **VARIATION** Sexes similar. **SIMILAR SPECIES** Pale Ranger (NW, Gau., Lim., Mpu., KZN, FS and Swa.) has black-edged white spots in underside hind wing. Chequered Ranger (N. Cape, NW, FS, Gau., Lim., Mpu., E. Cape) has no spots. Morant's (NW, Gau., Lim., Mpu., KZN) and the scarce Axehead (Lim.) oranges have small brown spots. **STATUS** Widespread but scarce.

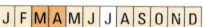

## Macken's Dart
Macken-se-dartelaartjie
*Acleros mackenii*  **27–33 mm**

**HABITS** Slow, low, skipping flight. Settles on plants in damp shady areas.
**HABITAT** Coastal bush and Afrotemperate forest. **EARLY STAGES Egg** a ribbed dome. Brownish-red. Laid singly on a leaf of *Bridelia micrantha*, *Combretum molle* or an *Acridocarpus* or *Terminalia*. **Larva** up to 18 mm. Cylindrical with neck-like narrowing behind head. Olive to pale green with dark oblique dorsolateral stripes. Shelter comprises leaves held together with silk. **Pupa** up to 13 mm. Head blunt and tail pointed. Proboscis sheath long and loose. Olive-green. Forms in larval shelter. **VARIATION** Sexually dimorphic, as shown. **SIMILAR SPECIES** The rare vagrant Common and White darts (Zimbabwe) are larger and lack underside hind wing striations. **STATUS** Locally common.

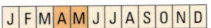

## Strelitzia Nightfighter
Strelitzia-skemervegter
*Moltena fiara*  **54–64 mm**

**HABITS** Fast, skipping flight close to food plants at dusk. ♂ makes clicking sound in flight. **HABITAT** Coastal bush. **EARLY STAGES Egg** a ribbed dome. Yellowish-green. Laid singly on a leaf of *Strelitzia nicolae*. **Larva** up to 65 mm. Cylindrical with neck-like narrowing behind head. Body pale green with red lateral stripes. Head whitish, outlined in black. Builds triangular shelter by cutting a slot in a leaf, folding it over and securing with silk. **Pupa** up to 32 mm. Elongated. Golden brown, covered in white powder. Forms in larval shelter. **VARIATION** Only ♂ has the white antennae. **SIMILAR SPECIES** Palm-tree Nightfighter (p. 144) ♂ has white on antenna tip only. ♀ has white streak on underside hind wing. **STATUS** Locally common.

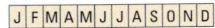

**HESPERIIDAE: HESPERIINAE / NIGHTFIGHTERS**

## Palm-tree Nightfighter
Palmboom-skemervegter
*Zophopetes dysmephila*     40–52 mm

**HABITS** Fast skipping flight close to food plants at dusk. ♂ territorial. **HABITAT** Coastal and riverine bush and forest, as well as urban gardens. **EARLY STAGES** *Egg* a ribbed dome. Pale brown. Laid singly on a leaf of *Phoenix reclinata* or on certain exotic palms. *Larva* up to 46 mm. Cylindrical with neck-like narrowing behind head. Body green with darker dorsal line. Head whitish-brown outlined in black. Constructs shelter of palm leaflets stitched with silk. *Pupa* up to 27 mm. Elongated. Golden brown, covered in white powder. Forms in larval shelter. **VARIATION** Only ♀ has white streak on underside hind wing. **SIMILAR SPECIES** Strelitzia Nightfighter (p. 135) ♂ has entirely white antennae. **STATUS** Locally common.

| J | F | M | A | M | J | J | A | S | O | N | D |

## Bush Nightfighter
Bos-skemervegter
*Artitropa erinnys erinnys*     53–63 mm

**HABITS** Fast skipping flight close to food plants at dusk. ♂ territorial. Both sexes fond of flowers. **HABITAT** Coastal and riverine bush. **EARLY STAGES** *Egg* a ribbed dome. White, turning pale brown. Laid singly on a leaf of a *Dracaena*. *Larva* up to 50 mm. Cylindrical with neck-like narrowing behind head. Body whitish-green with darker dorsal line. Head yellow with black spots. Constructs shelter by rolling a leaf and stitching it with silk. *Pupa* up to 31 mm. Elongated. Pale yellow-brown, covered in white powder. Forms in larval shelter. **VARIATION** Sexes similar. **SIMILAR SPECIES** Unique. **STATUS** Locally common.

| J | F | M | A | M | J | J | A | S | O | N | D |

## Peppered Hopper
**Gepeperde-springertjie**
*Platylesches ayresii*   **27–38 mm**

**HABITS** Fast, skipping flight close to the ground. Settles on low vegetation or rocks. ♂ defends hill-top territory. **HABITAT** Grassland and savanna. **EARLY STAGES** Details not recorded, but ♀ observed laying eggs on *Parinari capensis*. **VARIATION** Sexes similar. **SIMILAR SPECIES** Hilltop Hopper (NW, Gau., Mpu.) has similar underside hind wing, but upper side forewing has larger hyaline spots. Other hoppers lack the finely striated underside hind wing. **STATUS** Locally common.

| J | F | M | A | M | J | J | A | S | O | N | D |

## Honey Hopper
**Heuning-springertjie**
*Platylesches moritili*   **31–35 mm**

**HABITS** Fast, skipping flight. Settles on vegetation or rocks. Fond of flowers, particularly *Deinbollia oblongifolia*. **HABITAT** Warm savanna and riverine bush. **EARLY STAGES** *Egg* details not recorded. *Larva* up to 38 mm. Cylindrical with neck-like narrowing behind head. Body green. Head white with segmented brown pattern. Constructs shelter of *Parinari curatellifolia* leaves stitched with silk. *Pupa* up to 20 mm. Cream-white with brown marks. Forms in cocoon inside larval shelter. **VARIATION** Sexes similar. **SIMILAR SPECIES** Five similar hoppers are distinguished by pattern on underside hind wing. Variegated Acraea Hopper (Lim., northern KZN) has brightly coloured underside. Flower-girl Hopper (NW to KZN) most similar to Honey Hopper but has pale apex to underside forewing. **STATUS** Common and widespread.

| J | F | M | A | M | J | J | A | S | O | N | D |

## Orange-spotted Hopper
Oranje-springertjie
*Zenonia zeno*  34–41 mm

**HABITS** Fast skipping flight. Fond of flowers. ♂ highly aggressive and territorial. **HABITAT** Forest and riverine bush in savanna. **EARLY STAGES** Not recorded, but observed laying eggs on sorghum and maize. **VARIATION** Sexes similar. **SIMILAR SPECIES** Macomo Ranger (p. 142) and Pale (NW, Gau., Lim., Mpu., KZN, FS and Swa.) and Chequered (E. and N. Cape, NW, FS, Gau., Lim., Mpu.) rangers and the scarce Axehead Orange (Lim.) are similar on upper side, but only Orange-spotted Hopper has an underside hind wing pattern of large yellow blotches on a brown ground colour. **STATUS** Locally common.

## White-banded Swift
Witmerk-ratsvlieër
*Pelopidas thrax*  42–51 mm

**HABITS** Fast skipping flight. Fond of flowers. ♂ highly aggressive and territorial. **HABITAT** Woodlands and savanna. **EARLY STAGES** *Egg* a smooth dome. Yellow, turning salmon. Laid singly on a grass like *Imperata cylindrica*. *Larva* up to 45 mm. Cylindrical with neck-like narrowing behind head. Body green. Head white outlined in black. Constructs shelter of grass blades and silk. *Pupa* up to 29 mm. Elongated with pointed head. Body olive green. Head black. Forms inside larval shelter. **VARIATION** ♀ lacks white diagonal sex mark on upper side forewing. **SIMILAR SPECIES** Black-banded Swift has black sex mark. ♀ White-banded Swift may be confused with Long-horned (p. 147) and False (NW, Gau., Lim., Mpu., FS, KZ and Swa.) swifts but hyaline spots on upper side forewing are larger. **STATUS** Common and widespread.

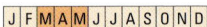

## Long-horned Swift
**Reënbos-ratsvlieër**
*Borbo fatuellus fatuellus*        33–43 mm

**HABITS** Fast skipping flight. Fond of flowers. **HABITAT** Coastal bush and savanna. **EARLY STAGES** *Egg* a smooth dome. Pale green. Laid singly on many grasses, or even maize. *Larva* up to 39 mm. Cylindrical with neck-like narrowing behind head. Body pale green with darker longitudinal stripes. Head white with black marks. Constructs larval shelter from grass and silk. *Pupa* up to 32 mm. Elongated with both ends pointed. Green with dark stripes on abdomen. Forms inside larval shelter. **VARIATION** Sexes similar. **SIMILAR SPECIES** Resembles eight other *Borbo* swifts, but only Lesser-horned (KZN) and Ferrous (northern KZN) swifts also lack spots in cell of upper side forewing. Ferrous Swift is red-brown, Lesser-horned Swift lacks pale markings and Dark Hottentot (eastern SA) has short antennae. **STATUS** Common and widespread.

## Common Hottentot
**Geel-hotnot**
*Gegenes niso niso*        29–35 mm

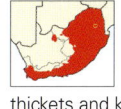

**HABITS** Fast, low, skipping flight. Settles often on grass stems. **HABITAT** Grassland and grass areas in forest, savanna, thickets and karoo vegetation. **EARLY STAGES** *Egg* a smooth dome. Pale yellow, turning green with pink spots. Laid singly on grasses. *Larva* up to 32 mm. Narrow, cylindrical with neck-like narrowing behind head. Pale green with dark longitudinal stripes. Constructs larval shelter from grass and silk. *Pupa* up to 16 mm. Elongated. Green with dark abdominal stripes. Forms inside larval shelter. **VARIATION** Sexually dimorphic, as shown. **SIMILAR SPECIES** ♂ Marsh Hottentot Skipper (absent from very arid areas) has black patch in upper side forewing. Water Watchman (eastern SA and Swa.) has plain underside hind wing with discal series of black spots (not dark-edged yellow blotches). **STATUS** Common and widespread.

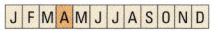

# GLOSSARY

**Abdomen** The third and hindmost portion of an insect's body, carrying the digestive system, genitalia, and excretory organs, is the softest and most vulnerable part of the body. It is visibly segmented.

**Alkaloid** A nitrogen-containing, often poisonous, organic compound derived from plants. The larvae and adults of some Lepidoptera can extract and store these substances that, though harmless to themselves, can be used as a defence against predators.

**Anal angle** The angle between the outer and inner margins of the hind wing. The corresponding angle on the forewing is the inner angle.

**Anal fold** The portion of the hind wing that covers the abdomen of the resting insect. Of vital importance in the flight mechanism of butterflies.

**Antennae** The feelers or elongated sensory organs attached to the heads of insects. In butterflies they are long, flexible and stick-like, pointing forwards, and the outer end is usually thickened or clubbed. They are organs of touch, smell, and taste.

**Apex** The point on the forewing where the costa and the outer margin meet.

**Apical** The area adjacent to the apex.

**Basal** In the wings, this is the portion nearest the thorax.

**Bifid** Divided into two parts.

**Caterpillar = larva** The form of a butterfly or moth that emerges from the egg.

**Cell (of wings)** An open wing area bounded by veins. This is situated at or near the base, and extends to the centre, of the wing.

**Chrysalis = pupa** An insect's pupal or third developmental stage before complete metamorphosis.

**Cilia** In butterflies, the fine fringe of small hairlike scales along the outer edges of the wings.

**Club** The thickened or swollen apical end of an antenna.

**Colony** A concentrated population of butterflies living in a small area confined by microclimate, vegetation, the presence of a host ant, or a combination of these and other factors.

**Common names** Vernacular names for butterflies. These names have no scientific significance.

**Costa** The leading edge or front margin of the fore- and hind wings.

**Countershading** Colour pattern that is darker on the upper side than the underside, providing camouflage.

**Dimorphism** An organism that may exist as one of two different forms. May describe differences between male and female (sexual dimorphism) or between seasonal forms (seasonal dimorphism).

**Disc** The central area of the wing.

**Discal area** The large central area of a wing, partly or completely bounded by ocellus.

**Dorsal** The upper surface or back.

**Endemic** A natural inhabitant of a particular geographic area.

**Eyespot** The false eye on the wing of an insect, or on the thorax of a caterpillar. Often has a dark pupil-like centre and is usually ringed with a contrasting colour. May be called an ocellus.

**Family** An assemblage of related genera. A taxonomic category ranking below an order and above a genus. The categories subfamily and tribe may also be used between a family and a genus.

**Food plant** The host plant on which Lepidopteran larvae feed.

**Form** A representative of a species that differs from the norm in some uniform character, and with which it interbreeds. Colour or shape variations may be constant. Environmental influences produce seasonal forms.

**Genus (pl. genera)** A group within a family consisting of one or more closely related species.

**Girdle** The silken strand spun as a sling around the thorax of certain butterfly pupae to allow them to hang horizontally or head upwards.

**Ground colour** The predominant colour of the wing.

**Haemolymph** The circulating body fluid of insects.

**Hair pencil** A dense tuft of specialised scale hairs on the body or wings of male butterflies, displayed during courtship. May carry pheromones to attract or excite the female.

**Hill-topping** The habit of some male butterflies of frequenting high areas, particularly during the hottest hours of the day.

**Hyaline** A transparent water-like colour.

**Instar** The larval period between the hatching of the egg and first moult (first instar), and the period between each successive moult until pupation. There are usually four to six instars before pupation.

**Larva (pl. larvae) = caterpillar** The sexually immature, feeding, developmental stage of an insect that undergoes complete metamorphosis.

**Lateral** Describing parts or features away from the midline, or on the side of an object.

**Lunule** A crescent-shaped marking or spot.

**Marginal** Describing features found on the outer margins of the wings.

**Mimic** An organism superficially resembling another of a different species, so that one or the other benefits.

**Nominate** The first of two or more subspecies in any species to be named.

**Ocellus** = Eyespot.

**Order** The major taxonomical subdivision of a phylum, e.g. the Insecta, into groups with similar basic characteristics. For example, all insects with wing scales are grouped in the order Lepidoptera.

**Outer margin** The distal or outer margin of a wing.

**Ovum (pl. ova)** Insect egg.

**Patrolling** Mate-location behaviour in which male butterflies fly almost continually, often along a repetitive beat, in search of females.

**Postdiscal** Describing features occupying the area between the discal and submarginal regions of the wing.

**Proboscis** A modified mouthpart of an insect. In Lepidoptera it is usually kept coiled like a watch spring. Butterflies have an entirely liquid diet and lack biting mouthparts. Some butterflies, such as the lycaenid genus *Thestor* (skollies), gain all their nutrition as larvae and so the adult proboscis is vestigial.

**Process(es)** A projection or protuberance.

**Pupa = chrysalis, chrysalid** The non-feeding, post-larval stage of complete metamorphosis.

**Race** Subspecies.

**Scales** The microscopic plates (actually flattened hairs) attached, like shingles on a roof, to the wing surfaces of Lepidoptera, which give the wings their colours and patterns.

**Seasonal dimorphism** Two distinct colour and/or size forms in a species, whose appearance depends on the season. Intermediate forms may occur between the two seasonal extremes.
**Segment** Ring-like or tubular section of the insect body or its appendages.
**Sex brand** Mark or patch on the wings of some male Lepidoptera.
**Sexual dimorphism** Genetically controlled phenomenon where males and females of the same species have a strikingly different appearance (form, colour or pattern).
**Spiracles** The external breathing holes of an insect, situated along the sides of the abdomen.
**Striated** Covered in striae, thin lines or bands.
**Subfamily** A section of a family containing genera more closely related to one another than to other genera in the family.
**Submarginal** The area of the wing between the margin and the postdiscal area.
**Subspecies** One or more taxonomically and geographically distinct populations or races of a species.
**Superfamily** A group of related families.
**Thorax** The intermediate region of the body, carrying the butterfly's legs and wings. It is the strongest and most rigid part of the body.

# INDEX TO SCIENTIFIC NAMES

*Abantis, paradisea* 137
   *venosa* 137
*Acleros mackenii* 143
*Acraea, acara acara* 40
   *acrita acrita* 38
   *aganice aganice* 36
   *anemosa* 41
   *boopis boopis* 38
   *caldarena caldarena* 39
   *horta* 37
   *natalica natalica* 39
   *oncaea* 40
   *petraea* 41
   *rabbaiae perlucida* 37
*Actizera lucida* 108
*Aeropetes tulbaghia* 25
*Afrodryas leda* 114
*Alaena amazoula* 69
*Alenia sandaster* 140
*Aloeides, aranda* 90
   *dentatis* 89
   *taikosama* 90
   *thyra* 89
*Amauris, albimaculata*
   *albimaculata* 21
   *echeria echeria* 22
   *niavius dominicanus* 20
   *ochlea ochlea* 21
*Anthene, amarah amarah* 94
   *definita definita* 94
   *dulcis dulcis* 95
   *larydas larydas* 95
*Aphnaeus hutchinsoni* 84
*Appias epaphia contracta* 124
*Argyraspodes argyraspis* 88
*Artitropa erinnys erinnys* 144
*Aslauga australis* 72
*Axiocerses, amanga amanga* 86
   *tjoane tjoane* 86
*Azanus, jesous* 109
   *moriqua* 110
   *natalensis* 110
*Baliochila aslanga* 70
*Belenois, aurota* 122
   *creona severina* 123
   *thysa thysa* 122
*Bicyclus, anynana anynana* 24
   *ena* 24
   *safitza safitza* 23
*Borbo fatuellus fatuellus* 147
*Byblia ilithyia* 60
*Cacyreus, lingeus* 96
   *marshalli* 97

*Capys, alpheus* 80
   *disjunctus* 81
*Cassionympha cassius* 30
*Catacroptera cloanthe cloanthe* 63
*Catopsilia florella* 112
*Celaenorrhinus mokeezi* 134
*Charaxes, achaemenes*
   *achaemenes* 53
   *brutus natalensis* 49
   *candiope candiope* 47
   *castor flavifasciatus* 49
   *cithaeron cithaeron* 51
   *druceanus* 50
   *etesipe tavetensis* 52
   *ethalion ethalion* 53
   *jahlusa* 52
   *jasius saturnus* 48
   *protoclea azota* 48
   *varanes varanes* 47
   *wakefieldi* 54
   *xiphares* 50
   *zoolina* 51
*Chilades trochylus* 111
*Chloroselas pseudozeritis*
   *pseudozeritis* 85
*Chrysoritis, natalensis* 91
   *nigricans* 92
   *thysbe* 92
   *zonarius* 91
*Cigaritis, mozambica* 85
   *natalensis* 84
*Cnodontes penningtoni* 71
*Coeliades, forestan forestan* 132
   *keithloa* 133
   *pisistratus* 133
*Coenyra hebe* 29
*Coenyropsis natalii* 32
*Colias electo electo* 112
*Colotis, annae annae* 118
   *antevippe gavisa* 119
   *auxo auxo* 119
   *celimene* 117
   *euippe omphale* 120
   *evagore antigone* 121
   *evenina evenina* 120
   *ione* 117
   *regina* 118
   *vesta argillaceus* 116
*Crudaria leroma* 93
*Cupidopsis cissus cissus* 107
*Cymothoe, alcimeda* 54
   *coranus* 55
*Danaus chrysippus orientis* 20

*Dingana dingana* 27
*Dira, clytus* 26
   *oxylus* 27
*Dixeia pigea* 123
*Durbania amakosa* 71
*Eicochrysops, hippocrates* 107
   *messapus* 106
*Eretis djaelaelae* 135
*Eronia cleodora* 114
*Euchrysops, malathana* 105
   *subpallida* 106
*Euphaedra neophron neophron* 56
*Eurema brigitta brigitta* 113
*Euryphura achlys* 55
*Eurytela, dryope angulata* 61
   *hiarbas angustata* 61
*Gegenes niso niso* 147
*Gnophodes betsimena diversa* 23
*Gomalia elma* 139
*Graphium, antheus* 131
   *leonidas leonidas* 130
   *morania* 130
   *policenes policenes* 131
   *porthaon porthaon* 132
*Hamanumida daedalus* 56
*Harpendyreus noquasa* 100
*Hemiolaus caeculus caeculus* 79
*Heteropsis perspicua perspicua* 25
*Hypolimnas, anthedon*
   *wahlbergi* 62
   *misippus* 62
*Hypolycaena, buxtoni buxtoni* 78
   *philippus philippus* 78
*Iolaus, bowkeri* 74
   *diametra natalica* 77
   *lulua* 75
   *mimosae* 77
   *pallene* 76
   *sidus* 76
   *silas* 75
*Junonia, hierta cebrene* 66
   *natalica natalica* 65
   *oenone oenone* 67
   *orithya madagascariensis* 67
   *terea elgiva* 66
*Kedestes, barberae* 141
   *macomo* 142
   *wallengrenii* 142
*Lachnocnema laches* 72
*Lachnoptera ayresii* 46
*Lampides boeticus* 99
*Lepidochrysops, asteris* 103
   *oreas* 102

*patricia* 103
*plebeia plebeia* 102
*praeterita* 101
*variabilis* 101
*Leptomyrina, gorgias gorgias* 80
  *hirundo* 79
*Leptosia alcesta inalcesta* 125
*Leptotes pirithous* 98
*Leucochitonea levubu* 136
*Libythea labdaca laius* 69
*Lycaena clarki* 93
*Melampias huebneri* 31
*Melanitis leda* 22
*Metisella metis* 140
*Moltena fiara* 143
*Mylothris, agathina agathina* 126
  *rueppellii haemus* 125
*Myrina, dermaptera dermaptera* 83
  *silenus* 83
*Neita neita* 31
*Nepheronia, argia* 115
  *buquetii buquetii* 115
  *thalassina sinalata* 116
*Neptis, laeta* 59
  *saclava marpessa* 58
*Netrobalane canopus* 136
*Orachrysops, ariadne* 104
  *niobe* 104
  *subravus* 105
*Oraidium barberae* 109
*Papilio, constantinus*
  *constantinus* 128
  *dardanus cenea* 127
  *demodocus demodocus* 128
*echerioides echerioides* 127
*euphranor* 126
*nireus lyaeus* 129
*ophidicephalus* 129
*Paralethe dendrophilus* 26
*Pardopsis punctatissima* 45
*Paternympha narycia* 34
*Pelopidas thrax* 146
*Pentila tropicalis* 70
*Phalanta phalantha aethiopica* 46
*Phasis thero* 87
*Physcaeneura panda* 30
*Pinacopteryx eriphia eriphia* 113
*Platylesches, ayresii* 145
  *moritili* 145
*Pontia helice helice* 124
*Precis, archesia* 64
  *octavia sesamus* 64
  *tugela tugela* 65
*Protogoniomorpha parhassus* 63
*Pseudacraea, boisduvalii trimenii* 57
  *eurytus imitator* 57
  *lucretia* 58
*Pseudonacaduba sichela sichela* 100
*Pseudonympha, magus* 33
  *poetula* 32
  *trimenii* 33
*Sarangesa motozi* 135
*Serradinga clarki* 28
*Sevenia, boisduvali boisduvali* 59
  *natalensis* 60
*Spialia, diomus ferax* 138
  *dromus* 138
  *spio* 139
*Stygionympha, vigilans* 34
  *wichgrafi* 35
*Tagiades flesus* 134
*Tarsocera cassus* 29
*Tarucus thespis* 99
*Telchinia, anacreon* 43
  *cabira* 44
  *encedon encedon* 45
  *esebria* 42
  *igola* 42
  *rahira rahira* 43
  *serena* 44
*Teracolus eris eris* 121
*Thestor, basutus* 74
  *protumnus* 73
  *yildizae* 73
*Torynesis mintha* 28
*Trimenia malagrida* 88
*Tsitana tsita* 141
*Tuxentius melaena* 98
*Tylopaedia sardonyx* 87
*Uranothauma nubifer* 96
*Vanessa, cardui* 68
  *hippomene hippomene* 68
*Virachola, antalus* 82
  *dinochares* 82
  *diocles* 81
*Ypthima, asterope* 36
  *impura paupera* 35
*Zenonia zeno* 146
*Zintha hintza* 97
*Zizeeria knysna knysna* 108
*Zizula hylax* 111
*Zophopetes dysmephila* 144

# INDEX TO AFRIKAANS COMMON NAMES

Arabier, Bont- 116
Asvlerkie, Suidelike- 72
Blaarvlerk, Rooi-en-blou- 64
  Rots- 64
  Tugela- 65
Blouglans 62
Bloutjie, Asvaal-
  dowwe- 106
  Brenton- 104
  Donker- 100
  Doringboom- 110
  Dubbelkol- 102
  Duweltjie- 108
  Dwerg- 109
  Gaika- 111
  Gewone-dowwe- 105
  Gewone-ertjie- 98
  Grou- 105
  Helder- 103
  Hemels- 109
  Hintza- 97
  Hoëveld- 101
  Karkloof- 104
  Kleinvyeboom- 83
  Koper- 106
  Lusern- 99
  Moeras-berg- 100
  Natalse- 110
  Patricia- 103
  Skiereiland- 102
  Verneuker- 101
  Vlei- 107
  Vyeboom- 83
  Witpunt-koper- 107
  Witstreep- 108
Bontetjie, Swart- 98
Boombruintjie, Boisduval-se- 59
  Natal- 60
Bosprag 26
Bosvlieër, Oranjelint- 61
  Witlint- 61
Bruintjie, Boland- 31
  Drakensberg- 32
  Geelband-skemer- 23
  Kloog- 34
  Natalse- 32
  Neita- 31
  Reënwoud-bos- 30
  Skeeloog-bos- 24
  Skemer- 22
  Spikkel-bos- 24
  Swart-bos- 23
  Tower- 33
  Trimen-se- 33
  Westelike-rant- 34
  Wichgraf-se-rant- 35
  Zoeloeskadu- 29
Dansertjie, Bos- 55
  Karoo- 140
  Skaduwee- 56
Dartelaartjie, Bruinpunt- 136
  Macken-se- 143
  Paradys- 137
  Skaduwee- 134
  Vos- 137
  Witjas- 136
Dubbelstert, Boskoning- 50
  Bosprins- 51
  Bosveld- 53
  Koppie- 48
  Kus- 53
  Pêrel- 47
  Reuse- 49
  Seldsame bos- 52
  Silwerkol- 52
  Silwerstreep- 50
  Skelm- 47
  Vlam- 48
  Wit-en-bruin- 51
  Witstreep- 49
Geelvlerkie, Natalse-boom- 70
  Pennington-se-boom- 71
  Spikkel- 70
Geletjie, Grasveld- 113
Gesiggie, Blou- 67
  Bos- 66
  Geel- 66
  Natal- 65
Hartbloutjie, Swart- 96
Hotnot, Geel- 147
Jagtertjie, Kersfeesbos- 134
Juweeltjie, Gras- 111
  Skitter- 85
Kaboutertjie, Motozi- 135
Klipsitter, Amakoza- 71
Kluisenaar, Marmer- 135
Koningin, Bos- 54
Konstabel, Dubbelkol- 133
  Rooibroek- 133

# INDEX TO AFRIKAANS COMMON NAMES / INDEX TO ENGLISH COMMON NAMES

Witbroek- 132
Kopertjie, Koning- 87
  Seldsame-berg- 88
  Vegter-silwerkol- 88
Kopervlerkie, Aranda- 90
  Donkie-madelief- 91
  Dowwe- 90
  Oostelike-klein- 93
  Roodepoort- 89
  Rooi- 89
Kortstertjie, Donker- 94
  Mashuna- 95
  Spikkel- 95
  Swartstreep- 94
Luiperd, Populier- 46
  Vaalkol- 46
Malvabloutjie 97
  Bos- 96
Monnik 20
Na-aper 62
Nooientjie, Berg- 25
  Suidelike-bos- 68
  Wit- 130
Opal, Bloujuweel- 92
  Natal- 91
  Prag- 92
Ouheks 21
Outannie 21
Papiertjie, Fladder- 125
Polkastippel 45
Pootjie, Suidelike bont-wol- 72
Puntjie, Bosveld-pers- 117
  Donkeroranje- 120
  Goud- 121
  Kleinoranje- 121
  Koningpers- 118
  Oranje- 120
  Rooioranje- 119
  Silwer-pyl- 87
  Skarlaken- 118
  Swaeloranje- 119
Quagga 113
Ratsvlieër, Reënbos- 147
  Witmerk- 146
Ringetjie, Afrikaanse- 36
  Gestreepte- 30
  Vuil- 35
Rokkie, Bont- 124
  Silwer- 84
  Sondags- 68
Rooitjie, Acara- 40
  Bloed- 41
  Boerbok- 42

Geelstreep- 44
Glasvlerk- 37
Kersboom- 41
Kleinoranje- 44
Moeras- 43
Natal- 39
Oranje- 43
Reënwoud- 38
Rooibokkie- 40
Swartbont- 36
Swartpunt- 39
Tuin- 37
Vuilvenster- 42
Vuur- 38
Witstreep- 45
Rooivlerkie, Bos- 86
  Ralie- 86
Saffier, Bowker-se-marmer- 74
  Doringboom- 77
  Geel- 76
  Natalsegeelstreep- 77
  Rooistreep- 76
  Suidelike 75
  Witkol- 75
Sandmannetjie, Berg- 139
  Bos- 138
  Gewone- 138
Seerower 63
Skemervegter, Bos- 144
  Palmboom- 144
  Strelitzia- 143
Skoenlapper, Lemoen- 128
  Lusern- 112
  Melkbos- 20
  Perlemoen- 63
  Snuit- 69
Skollie, Basoetoe- 74
  Boland- 73
  Skiereiland- 73
Spelertjie, Bruin- 82
  Oranje- 82
  Skaduwee- 81
Spikkelbloutjie, Fynbos- 99
Springertjie, Asjas- 139
  Gepeperde- 145
  Heuning- 145
  Oranje- 146
Stertbloutjie, Buxton-se- 78
  Persbruin- 78
  Venda-se- 79
Streepvlerkie, Mosambiek- 85
  Natalse- 84
Suikerbossie, Oranjeband- 80

Sannie-se- 81
Swaardstert, Bont- 130
  Jag- 131
  Kwagga- 132
  Ooskus- 131
Swaelstert, Groenlint- 129
  Koning- 129
  Konstantyn-se- 128
  Na-aper 127
  Vlieëndepiering- 126
  Witlint- 127
Swartogie, Gewone- 80
  Langstert- 79
Swerwer, Afrikaanse 112
  Blou- 116
  Buquet- 115
  Druiweblaar- 114
  Groot 115
  Herfsblaar- 114
  Reënbos- 59
  Spikkel- 58
Tarentaaltjie 56
Toordokter 22
Valetjie, Spikkel- 93
Valsrooitjie, Bont- 58
  Skaduwee- 57
  Trimen-se- 57
Vegter, Leliegras 60
Verneukertjie 62
Wagter, Boom- 117
  Moeras- 25
Wagtertjie-, Pad 67
  Barber-se- 141
  Macomo- 142
  Wallengren-se- 142
Walsertjie, Donker- 141
  Reënbos- 140
Weduwee, Clark-se- 28
  Dingaan-se- 27
  Kaapse-herfs- 26
  Lente- 29
  Mintha- 28
  Pondoland- 27
Witjie, Afrikaanse gewone 123
  Gewone voëlent- 126
  Grasveld- 123
  Miershoop- 123
  Oranjevlerk voëlent- 125
  Vals- 122
  Willa- 124
Witkoppie, Alsie- 54
  Cora- 55
Zoeloe, Geel- 69

# INDEX TO ENGLISH COMMON NAMES

Acraea, Acara 40
  Black-tipped 39
  Blood-red 41
  Broad-bordered 41
  Clear-wing 37
  Dancing 44
  Dusky 42
  Dusky-veined 42
  Fiery 38
  Garden 37
  Marsh 43
  Natal 39
  Orange 43
  Rainforest 38

Trimen's False 57
White-barred 45
Window 40
Yellow-banded 44
Admiral, Southern Short-tailed 68
Arrowhead, Silver 87
Bar, Mozambique 85
  Natal 84
Beauty, Forest 26
  Table Mountain 25
Black-eye, Common 80
  Tailed 79
Blue, African Grass 108
  Ashen Smoky 106

Black-bordered Babul 110
Brenton 19
Brilliant 103
Common Fig-tree 83
Common Meadow 107
Common Smoky 105
Common Zebra 98
Cupreous 106
Dwarf 109
Grizzled 105
Highveld 101
Karkloof 104
Lesser Fig-tree 83
Marsh Mountain 100

# INDEX TO ENGLISH COMMON NAMES

Natal Babul 110
Patricia 103
Pea 99
Peninsula 102
Rayed 108
Tiny Grass 111
Topaz Babul 109
Twin-spot 102
Variable 101
Vivid Dotted 99
White-tipped 107
Bronze, Bush 96
  Common Geranium 97
Brown, Boland 31
  Common Bush 23
  Drakensberg 32
  Eyed Bush 25
  Grizzled Bush 24
  Natal 32
  Neita 31
  Rainforest 30
  Silver-bottom 33
  Spotted-eye 34
  Squinting Bush 24
  Trimen's 33
  Twilight 22
  Western Hillside 34
  Wichgraf's Hillside 35
  Yellow-banded Evening 23
Buff, Natal 70
  Pennington's 71
Butterfly, Guinea-fowl 56
Charaxes, Blue-spotted 51
  Bushveld 53
  Club-tailed 51
  Flame-bordered 48
  Forest-king 50
  Foxy 48
  Giant 49
  Green-veined 47
  Pearl 47
  Pearl-spotted 52
  Satyr 53
  Scarce Forest 52
  Silver-barred 50
  White-barred 49
Chief 22
  False 58
Commodore, Brown 65
  Dead-leaf (Eared) 65
  Garden 64
  Gaudy 64
Copper, Aranda 90
  Donkey Daisy 91
  Dusky 90
  Eastern Sorrel 93
  King 87
  Red 89
  Roodepoort 89
  Scarce Mountain 88
  Warrior Silver-spotted 88
Dancer, Karoo 140
Dart, Macken's 143
Diadem, Common 62
  Variable 62
Dotted Border, Common 126
  False 122
  Twin 125
Elf, Marbled 135
Forester, Christmas 134
  Clouded 134
  Gold-banded 56

Friar 20
Gem, Brilliant 85
Glider, Battling 54
  Blonde 55
Grey, Silver-spotted 93
Hairstreak, Azure 79
  Buxton's 79
  Purplebrown 78
Hairtail, Black Striped 94
  Common 94
  Mashuna 95
  Spotted 95
Handkerchief, Flying 127
Heart, Black 96
Highflier, Hutchinson's 84
Hopper, Honey 145
  Orange-spotted 146
  Peppered 145
Hottentot, Common 147
Jewel, Grass 111
Joker, Spotted 60
Lady, Painted 68
  White 130
Layman 21
Lineblue, Dusky 100
Leopard, African 46
  Blotched 46
Migrant, African 112
Monarch, African 20
Mother-of-pearl 63
Nightfighter, Bush 144
  Palm-tree 144
  Strelitzia 143
Novice 21
Nymph, Mottled-
  green 55
Opal, Common 92
  Dark 92
  Natal 91
Pansy, Blue 67
  Eyed 67
  Soldier 66
  Yellow 66
Pentila, Spotted 70
Pie, Black 98
Pierrot, Hintza 97
Piper, Golden 61
  Pied 61
Pirate 63
Playboy, Apricot 82
  Brown 82
  Orange-barred 81
Policeman, Red-tab 133
  Striped 132
  Two-pip 133
Polka Dot 45
Protea, Orange Banded 80
  Russet 81
Purple, Southern 72
Queen, Forest 54
Ranger, Barber's 141
  Macomo 142
  Wallengren's 142
Ringlet, African 36
  Dark-webbed 30
  Impure 35
Rocksitter, Amakosa 71
Sailer, Common 59
  Spotted 58
Sandman, Common 138
  Forest 138
  Mountain 139

Sapphire, Bowker's Marbled 74
  Mimosa 77
  Natal Yellow-banded 77
  Red-line 76
  Saffron 76
  Southern 75
  White-spotted 75
Scarlet, Bush 86
  Eastern 86
Shadefly, Zulu 29
Skipper, Buff-tipped 136
  Elfin 135
  Green-marbled 139
  Paradise 137
  Veined 137
  White-cloaked 136
Skolly, Basuto 74
  Boland 73
  Peninsula 73
Snout, African 69
Swallowtail, Bush Kite 126
  Citrus 128
  Constantine's 128
  Emperor 129
  Green-banded 129
  Mocker 127
  White-banded 127
Swift, Long-horned 147
  White-banded 146
Swordtail, Cream-striped 132
  Large Striped 131
  Small Striped 131
  Veined 130
Sylph, Dismal 141
  Gold-spotted 140
Tip, Banded Gold 121
  Bushveld Purple 117
  Common Orange 120
  Lilac 117
  Queen Purple 118
  Red 119
  Scarlet 118
  Small Orange 121
  Smoky Orange 120
  Sulphur Orange 119
  Veined 116
Tree Nymph, Boisduval's 59
  Natal 60
Vagrant, Autumn-leaf 114
  Buquet's 115
  Cambridge 116
  Large 115
  Vine-leaf 114
Wanderer 36
  False 57
White, African Common 123
  African Wood 125
  Ant-heap 123
  Brown-veined 122
  Common Meadow 124
  Diverse Albatross 124
  Zebra 113
Widow, Cape Autumn 26
  Clark's 28
  Dingaan's 27
  Mintha 28
  Pondoland 27
  Spring 29
Woolly Legs, Southern Pied 72
Yellow, African Clouded 112
  Broad-bordered Grass 113
Zulu, Yellow 69